Endless Connections
Taking God's Word to Heart

Sister Jane Eschweiler, sds

Endless Connections
Taking God's Word to Heart

Jane Eschweiler, S.D.S.

Sheed & Ward
Kansas City

Sheed & Ward™ is a service of The National Catholic Reporter Publishing Company.

Library of Congress Cataloguing-in-Publication Data
Eschweiler, Jane, 1947-
　　Endless connections : taking God's word to heart / Jane Eschweiler.
　　　　p.　cm.
　　Includes index.
　　ISBN 1-55612-915-7 (alk. paper)
　　　1. Catholic Church—Sermons.　2. Sermons, American.
　I. Title.
　BX1756.E74E53　1997
　252¹.02—dc21　　　　　　　　　　　　　　　　　　97-8944
　　　　　　　　　　　　　　　　　　　　　　　　　　　　CIP

Published by:　Sheed & Ward
　　　　　　　115 E. Armour Blvd.
　　　　　　　P.O. Box 419492
　　　　　　　Kansas City, MO 64141-6492

To order, call: (800) 333-7373

www.natcath.com/sheedward

Illustrations and cover design by Jane Pitz.

Contents

III. Advent Musings

IV. Christmas and Other Such Gifts

V. Glimpses from that Extraordinary Ordinary Time

VI. Prophetic Challenges

VII. Lenten Reflections

VIII. Celebrating the Risen Jesus

IX. Special Feasts and Themes

X. What Kingdom People Do

Acknowledgments

This book represents the shared faith experience of many communities to which I have been connected. I am grateful to my family and friends, the Sisters of the Divine Savior, the parishes of St. Francis in Booneville, Mississippi; St. Mary's, in Iuka, Mississippi; and St. Andrew in Saginaw, Michigan, in which these homilies were born and delivered, and the Sisters of Charity of the Blessed Virgin Mary, with whom I lived while preparing this collection.

Special thanks to Carol Frances Jegen, BVM, of Loyola University's Institute for Pastoral Studies who carefully and lovingly mentored this project, as well as Margaret Shekleton, SDS and Margaret Bosch, SDS, who proofread the manuscript in its later stages. Finally, I am grateful to all those persons who have enhanced my appreciation of God's Word.

Introduction

Catholics are insisting on *good preaching* today! And they have a right. Whether their insistence on quality homilies comes in the form of "parish shopping" or specific feedback to their homilists, worshippers are demanding that the Word of God be proclaimed as *alive and well* in their communities.

And how does good preaching happen? It doesn't just happen! A quality homily in the Catholic tradition, or a constructive sermon in the wider Christian tradition, is a work of study, prayer, formulation, revision, more prayer, and hopefully conversation with the people or experiences of the community who will be sharing the message. I have called the week before delivering a homily "having a homily inside me" and the feeling is akin to midwifery in many ways! I tinker with introductions, tamper with images, wonder about the best closure, and worry about the length as I drive the car, visit the sick, or wait for a cheeseburger. Often that week, I am unusually moved by how people express grace in their lives, and sometimes their observations make their way into my text.

A good homily is a *memorable* homily. Whether it engages the listener with a verse from a country song, a line from a popular movie, a reminder of a headline or television newscast, it must invite the community to interface the *Word* with the *World of their experience* and provide new insight for action. I remember launching a homily with a story from my own life that had touched me deeply and having a woman approach me several years later with her memory of it. My story, a particular event in one individual's life, had reflected her story, and hopefully something that finds its way into everyone's story.

And when blended with eyes of faith and the loving memory of Jesus, such encounters can be exciting!

Homilies that are memorable are *helpful*. They create a world in which the believer can walk around in the space that Scripture provides and try on the attitude of prophet, leper, Pharisee or Jesus Himself . . . and feel again the power of God saving. This is Good News!

If I were to sit with a group of people interested in becoming good preachers, I would encourage them to be conscious of two essential elements every time they prepare a homily. First, I would urge them to *inspire:* to awaken, to startle, to awe, to comfort, or to quicken the sensitivities of their listeners. This involves both creativity and awareness of the life and experience of the community with whom one shares the Word. It also demands a compassionate understanding of human nature with all its warts and wonders! Grace is operative when events as presented surprise, when concepts as imagined comfort, and when stories as unfolded reveal!

Second, the homily needs to *challenge* the community; that is, it must urge their movement from this moment to the future with some new attitude, some greater energy, some deeper motivation, or some greater inclusivity. A preacher who always comforts but never challenges might be popular but not entirely faithful to the Word that she or he is privileged to share.

The collection of homilies that follows is a harvest of eight years of preaching (1987-1995) in the dioceses of Jackson, Mississippi and Saginaw, Michigan while I served as pastoral administrator and pastoral associate on holy ground. They represent a variety of approaches to proclaiming the Word of God in a way that sought to comfort and challenge. Some of these have been adapted for wider ecumenical use, but most represent an effort to be faithful to liturgical seasons and moods of the Church year.

Years after I began preaching, I found a description of the art by Frederick Buechner of the Presbyterian tradition in his spiritual autobiography entitled *Telling Secrets*. It speaks of the dynamic and engaging process I have witnessed frequently and experienced myself on occasion:

> I had never understood so clearly before what preaching is to me. Basically, it is to proclaim a Mystery before which, before whom, even our most exalted ideas turn to straw. It is also to proclaim this Mystery with a passion that ideas alone have little to do with. It is to try to put the Gospel into words not the way you would compose an essay but the way you would write a poem or a love letter—putting your heart into it, your own excitement, most of all your own life. It is to speak words that you hope may, by grace, be bearers not simply of new understanding but of new life both for the ones you are speaking to and also for you. Out of that life, who knows what new ideas about peace and honesty and social responsibility may come (p. 61).

But this book is not for preachers alone! Every component of good preaching is equally present in the formation of a solid *Christian spirituality*. So let me re-visit my remarks on good preaching in a way that enlarges the conversation to include all of us seeking life and spirit.

How does good spirituality happen? It *doesn't just happen*! It results from our study, reflection, prayer, and conversation with others who share our journey. It's a way of living life that opens any of our experiences to the possibility of a visit by the Sacred! We "spiritual" people find God alive and well in any graced moment of life: when we ask deep questions of our experiences, when we are saddened by the presence of violence, or when we are amused by the delight that a change of weather, a child's innocent words, or the renderings of an artist can produce! All of these are words of God in our world of experience that provide stories to continue the loving memory of Jesus in a dynamic encounter of love, tragedy, and relationship. The homilies in this book provide samples of how that can happen.

Spirituality is unleashed when our awareness, knowledge, and love interact to propel experience into insight and encounter into commitment. Spirituality is shared when your experience resonates with my story and we can help each other interpret them in light of the *universal love story* of God's creative acts, Jesus' saving presence, and the dynamic energy of the Spirit. This process requires trust and imagination, a willingness to sit with our experience long enough to let it startle us, and the confidence that what we glean from it could be encouraging to another. The enclosed homilies taught me that our stories will only be private storehouses of memory until they are shared in the context of faith. Only then can their meaning be explored and their gift of fruitfulness be received.

Finally, spirituality keeps us moving, challenging our complacency and comforting our broken places. What we learn we share. And what we share prompts *decisive action*. Note the titles of chapter ten's offerings. We need to stay haunted by the holy, choose adventure rather than monotony, include others or be excluded from God's reign, and live with ambivalence as we stand by Jesus, our God-send. Good homilies aid spirit-filled people toward loving witness and responsible action. Hopefully this book will advance the growing interest in good preaching and inspire the kind of reflection needed for solid Christian spirituality in each of us who wants to stay alive and well!

DON'T SETTLE FOR WATER WHEN THERE'S WINE
DON'T SETTLE FOR WATER WHEN THERE'S WINE
DON'T SETTLE FOR WATER WHEN THERE'S WINE

DON'T SETTLE FOR WATER WHEN THERE'S WINE

COMPANIONS FOR LIFE

STRANGERSNEIGHBORS
neighborsstrangers
BUILD-BRIDGES
NEIGHBORS&STRANGERS

break through the barrier
the barrier break through

KISSER KISSED
KISS
GOD'S NATURE IS INCLUSIVE

inclusive
constant
faithful
FRESH

ABOUT LOVE, ALL KINDS OF LOVE

1.

Why Can't All Strangers Be as Lovable as E.T.?

Exodus 22:20-26
Matthew 22:34-40

You have probably heard the motto: "We are shaped by those who have loved us and those who have refused to love us." Today our first and Gospel readings show us what happens in both cases! In our reading from the Book of Exodus, the Israelites are read their duties to strangers, to the poor, to displaced persons: in today's terms, aliens. They're reminded that they, too, were once strangers, wandering in Egypt. They're asked to remember how it felt. And the rule is: You keep getting milk and honey if you keep sharing it! If not, you lose yours, too! You might have seen a recent Bill Cosby scenario where his neighbor nearly disowned him over a very coveted drill! There are so many examples of this dynamic, this challenge, every day.

Let's consider the notion of *stranger*. Sometimes we want to be strangers, anonymous, so we won't have to get involved. But most times it's good to be greeted, recognized, and known by name because it brings happiness in belonging. Usually our experience of being the stranger is temporary.

Many times, our judgment of the "stranger" is negative. Without even meaning to, we can feel "they" can't be trusted. Maybe the only one we've liked in years is E.T., the ever-present extra-terrestrial who won the hearts of millions of moviegoers.

So maybe it's important to go back to our brief moments of feeling like strangers. Teens say they don't want to go someplace because they won't know anyone there. Adults sometimes say they need a few drinks before feeling confident at the office Christmas party. Couples often share that they have grown tired of each other, come to a stage of boredom, feel almost invisible, and finally like strangers in the house.

Let's be honest. It's easy to love those we know love us. But that's not even half the requirement here. God could have seen to it that in every situation all have enough because there is enough for all. Instead, sometimes God seems to plan that we share with and need each other. Sometimes God allows us to experience the *other* side: feeling lost like orphans, lonely like recent widows, alienated like refugee families. This is so we become sensitive to those who know those feelings a lot.

To the Jews, all but Jews were strangers. Most were invaders, plunderers, oppressors. And Yahweh tells them, "If you're like Me, you're full of compassion!" Think of the history of immigration in the United States, especially from 1870 to 1910 or so. The Statue of Liberty reads, "Give me your tired, your poor, your huddled masses. . . ." But we mocked the language and customs of these immigrants when we forgot God's inclusive nature. It is wonderful that the Church is now providing sanctuary for some families threatened by terrorist regimes. That's more like it.

Our Gospel today assures us that loving neighbor as self is as important as love of God. The logic seems to be that if God is the common origin of us all, then everyone who calls God the source of life is brother and sister. Relationships, then, arise out of love of God. And it is these *relationships* that provide the greatest thrill and the greatest pain in life.

Remember Mary Magdalen's haunting lyric in *Jesus Christ, Superstar?* She was referring to Jesus when she said, "I don't know how to love Him." There's not one of us here who doesn't struggle with this: how to express it, how to extend it, how to break through the barriers and walls that the stigma "stranger" throws up between God's people.

I have often been inspired by visits from parishioners who came not to gossip about fellow church members but to explore how we can better reach out, how we can make strangers into friends. This is the spirit of the Good News today; this is a picture of what God looks like. We would be mistaken to water down this message or pamper ourselves by not applying it practically.

This mandate says, "Take religion out of the church! Take love into the warehouse, the computer store, the barn, the classroom, and every corner of your house!" This command says to the very married, "Build bridges! Meet each other half way!" It calls to the teen: "Take the risk! Enlarge your circle of friends!" It warns the gossip: "Add a positive after that curt remark!"

We have been shaped by the God and the good people who have loved us. They made us neighbors, friends, spouses, trusted co-workers. Keeping that gift in mind, we can attest to the fact that E.T. is not the only lovable stranger Jesus requires us to accept as completely as we do ourselves! Maybe we *do* know how to love Him after all!

2.

Do We Really Need an Adversary?: Jesus on Love of Enemies

Matthew 6:27-38

If we could choose one command we wish Jesus had never given, it'd probably be *love your enemies*. Some people say they have none, yet I'll bet there are times they spot people going up one aisle in the grocery and decide to take the next. Or, they'd rather have the flu for a week than sit next to a certain relative at a wedding reception! Our adrenaline tells us when we've been attacked, want to retreat, or just can't cope, and retaliation is the most natural way to protect and defend ourselves.

Since Jesus fully shared our nature, He understood and experienced adrenaline! He knew that, human nature being what it is, we seem to *need* adversaries. We just can't seem to live without encountering conflict.

Look at Scripture: from Cain and Abel on, there's enmity! Christian religions did not condemn the institution of slavery as morally wrong until the mid nineteenth century, yet the enmities that were created were mammoth in proportion! The church's "Just War Theory" told us for years that it was OK to kill a perceived enemy as long as the conflict met seven criteria. Our forms of entertainment pit one team or player against another in exciting adversity and, based on the color of the uniform, we wish one or the other group defeat! Once one country is no longer our worst foe, another takes its place. Recently a local Chevrolet dealer allowed the public to come to his used car lot and literally trash a car made with Japanese parts: a gruesome and violent sport, it seemed to me. Imagine a presidential primary without reputations slain and mud slung! And imagine a day when people would refrain from putting other people down . . . and maybe even more amazing, a day we didn't put ourselves down as the worst enemy! In short, we make enemies and thrive on adversarial dynamics.

Now Jesus didn't say we wouldn't have enemies. He said pray for them and learn to love them. Our response can be, "Did He really *mean* it?" or "It's *impossible!*" But He meant it and gives us the help we need not to retaliate. And we have role models to show us love of enemy is possible!

First, a humorous example. An elder told me when she goes to her grandson's games, she wants him to win but cheers when a player on the opposing team makes a brilliant play! Now *she* looks beyond the uniform!

The *Saginaw News* reported recently that the mother of one of Jeffrey Dahmer's victims got up in Milwaukee County Court and said, "I don't hate him." Her healing started the moment she crossed the *we/they* line with remarkable mercy!

Terry Anderson was chained, abused, and separated from family for six and a half years, and the day after his release he told the people of America: "I am Christian and Catholic. It is required of me that I forgive, no matter how hard, and I am determined to do that." This disposition echoes infinitely more than toleration, which is usually enough for most of us!

The Greek word for *love* which Jesus uttered in the "love of enemy" passage does not translate passion for a spouse, nor does it imply affection for closest kin. What it means is an active desire that the best happen to the enemy, as well as a commitment to go out of one's way to be kind to her or him. All other rabbis and wisdom figures including Confucius put the Golden Rule of reciprocity in the negative, but Jesus gives us a *positive ethic* of non-retaliation. And He suggests we start by praying that good will come to the adversary. Often this helps us re-view the person as more *like* us than different. And this is the cutting edge of the Gospel.

This Gospel, then, leaves us with more questions than "Did He mean it?" The bottom line is, "Can any of us really let go of needing an adversary?" If we could, we really would leave vengeance to God alone. Wouldn't it be a relief to let God handle it? Or would it be disappointing because God would be more merciful to our enemies than we could? Can we trust a mercy that radical?

Andy Rooney has written, "We make more friends than we have time to keep, but we make more enemies than we have time to fight, so it all evens out." For the Christian, the goal is not to even the score but to do what is required and receive a spectacular promise: God's mercy will be returned to us as lavishly as we pour it out on others!

3.

Who Isn't My Neighbor?: Another Look at the Good Samaritan

Luke 10:25-37

Those who study the development of the human person say that there are certain questions we grapple with at every stage of our lives: First, "Who am I? How do I fit in?" These are related to identity issues. Then, "With whom do I want to be?" This is an intimacy concern. And finally, the philosophical question that haunts us the rest of our lives: "What gives my life meaning?" All three are related to the question in today's Gospel parable: *Who is my neighbor?* The answer to that last question affects who I am, who I am with, and what makes sense. That is, all three of the life development issues that envelop our experiences and prompt our growth.

Think back on the last five years: where you've lived and worked, where you've shopped, whom you've visited, new friends and neighbors. Circumstances have changed! There are new folks at your job sites, new neighbors next door, perhaps a new boss, and certainly new faces among your children's school friends. You have constantly responded to new *neighbors*. Yesterday's may not be today's. And some are easier to accept than others.

Neighborliness, or hospitality, is the most convincing sign that we are Christian, that we are what we profess to be. Jesus uses a memorable story to teach about the cost of neighborliness, one that we've heard often and can picture vividly. All the professional pray-ers and higher-ups pass a half-dead person on the road. But it's the enemy of the Jews, the Samaritan, who ironically is labeled "good" by the Master Teacher because it is the Samaritan that passes the ultimate test of neighborliness: treating the wounded stranger as kin and sacrificing time, money, safety, and convenience so that his quality of life is assured. His *heart* is moved. His mind might have registered, "I am needed," but his heart is stirred to perform no less kindness for this one than for his own family. It does not appear that Jesus wants his response to measure the considerations of what this will involve. No, He responds like the God who makes us all kin: noticing, carrying, nursing, paying, and, yes, staying. And then the "besides" gesture: If there is anything else . . . Count on me. This is where our belief might be stretched to the limit: "He's too good!" But the story illustrates what it was that Jesus asked: love another just as tenderly, just as carefully, just as thoroughly as you love your own self . . . and as I love you.

The Samaritan-Jew distinction, this we/they categorizing of who's friend, who's enemy, who's in and therefore who's left out, exists as strongly today. Just last week a middle-aged woman called me just to have a church-person listen. But before she got too far, she said, "I'm Black. Will you still listen?" This brought home to me once again how society has determined for certain groups who the strangers are. And they feel it. Sometimes it's widows or single parents who are left out. Sometimes the teens who aren't able to afford designer jeans, purses, shoes. And again, we are faced with the question: *Who is my neighbor?* And Jesus is heard answering, "Not just the one next door!"

The kind of response the Good Samaritan gave is repeated by our parishioners when I call to ask them to help with some specific need. Frequently I hear, "Yes. And what else can we do?" And I am inspired every time!

As I was completing this homily, reflecting on the lesson that "All God's people are my kinfolk," a pair of Jehovah Witnesses rang the doorbell ready to evangelize me. Despite my admission that I myself am a church minister, they persisted. And then my own words convicted me: "All God's people are my kinfolk!" Sometimes Jesus' sense of humor hits awfully close to home . . . in fact, at home!

4.

STREISANd ANd JESUS: PEOPLE WHO NEEd PEOPLE

John 17:11b-19

Parents are sometimes confronted by a child who excitedly reports, "So-and-so said such-and-such!" and the message is so unbelievable that the parent is forced to ask when, where, and to whom questions about the information! We need to know the situation in which words are spoken to understand their meaning and the intention of the speaker.

A good example of this is today's Gospel passage. It is a portion of Jesus' farewell discourse, or priestly prayer, which the writer of John's Gospel places in the context of the Last Supper scene before Jesus' arrest. It's as though we are given the privilege of eavesdropping on this faithful Son's intimate conversation with God before His agony and death!

What do we learn? One thing is that Jesus prayed from the heart . . . and for others. He prays here like a parent who has done all she or he could do for the child and now has to let go but still begs for the child's protection and total good. We might do well to ask ourselves how honest our prayer is. Sometimes without meaning to, we try to impress the God Who knows us so well instead of sharing from deep down what is really going on. And do we regularly pray for others, another admirable quality in Jesus' prayer? If we do engage in intercessory prayer, do we have at heart others' happiness, or subtly hope they will conform their will or life or decisions to ours?

Another gift we receive from witnessing Jesus' relationship with God is His priority of *unity*. His concern at the end—and all the way through His time with the disciples—is that they become one on the deepest possible level, that of faith and commitment. I can relate to this deep desire of Jesus when I realize that I am happiest when we as a parish family experience times of oneness, of harmony. This doesn't mean denying the diversity among us but trying to see and say the good about each member and really celebrating that! I have often seen our unity become a gift to our guests, and this warms my heart every time! It makes me glad to be here!

The Gospel scenario we cherish today is a proof to me that Jesus knows our *need* for community. Barbra Streisand may sing the now classic line, "People who need people are the luckiest people in the world." But another person of her Jewish ancestry said it with His whole life and ministry! And the unhappiness of blind legalism and selfishness in His world and our own arise not from folks who know they need others but from those who claim they don't.

But lest we glamorize unity too unrealistically, we need to remember that community is not merely a pool of good feelings, just as prayer is not. It is rather the forum and gathering place of gifts, the place where sharing is a way of life, a sharing that goes beyond the parameters of the church property! And joy is the sign of that community, the kind of joy Jesus tells His friends He wants them to know deeply and completely.

Last week one night I fell asleep with such a satisfying, spiritual joy. It was because I had been among you, and saw again how you love to be together and bring your goodness to so many others.

One last farewell theme Jesus prays about in our Gospel is guarding those He has loved from the evil one, a plea He makes to God on their, on our, behalf. If we were to name the presence of the evil one, we might think of cults, witchcraft, overt acts of violence or betrayal, the prevalence of unfaithfulness, or the hypocrisy of people trying to be what they're not. But the evil that corrodes and obstructs unity is any attitude or action that denies the dream of Jesus: that all, that *all*, be one. That means a world of people who need people. We who work for that are the luckiest people in the world!

5.

The Importance of a Prepositional Phrase: Self-love in the Gospel of Matthew

Matthew 22:38-40

A principal who supervised my teaching ability once remarked she never saw anyone get so excited over prepositional phrases! One day she watched me trying to convince high school sophomores of their importance. I stressed that they can make all the difference in what we understand and value in the communication dynamic. For example, "The ceiling (above me) is caving in!" carries more immediate excitement than the bland "The ceiling (in this picture) is caving in." What a difference a preposition makes!

In the Gospel today, Jesus reduces the 248 commands and 365 prohibitions of the Torah—the Jewish Law—into our two great commandments, and we can't afford to neglect a very important prepositional phrase: *"as yourself."* We can only hope to love God and neighbor as well as we love ourselves. And just maybe the neighbor we need to love, the neglected stranger, is *us*!

What about this very important, somewhat awkward topic of self-love? Let's spend a few moments considering it. Some time ago, I attended a workshop on self-esteem. When I got there, I looked around the room and figured I probably valued myself at least as much as the others in attendance. But as we were led through various exercises, I was surprised to discover how many ways I don't! I was easily able, for instance, to list physical and character traits I do not accept about myself, a list longer than I had expected!

By now some of us are probably thinking this is a psychological talk, not a homily. And maybe a few of us will only consider self-love a *virtue* when Jesus demands it! Certainly what we are not talking about is self-centered living, snobbery, ego-tripping, or denying our faults! But the fact is, we need to try to see ourselves as God sees us, as the very *likeness* of God, that is, lovable and capable of loving.

Now somewhere along the way, our view of ourselves became crippled or was wounded, to a greater or lesser degree. But we are the apple of God's eye, not the worm that spoils the apple!

My favorite television show one season a few years back was "The Trials of Rosie O'Neill." It shatters our image of which people do and do not, can and cannot, love themselves properly. First we see Rosie talking about her fears, guilt, and insecurities with a counselor, then witness her competence as a city attorney! Appearances can fool us!

How did we get this way? And why don't we love ourselves completely as Jesus asks? Some of us were taught to be perfect and can never measure up so are never satisfied! Some of us heard negative messages early on in our lives. I have a next door neighbor child that may as well be an abused house pet. He hears nothing but loud commands and name-calling from his parents. Another possible explanation is our religious training, at least those of us who can remember the pre-Vatican II style! We were taught that the correct sequence for love was God, then others, and if there's time or energy, *me*! Now how many times have any of us felt we *sinned* by not loving ourselves? Would any of you here who has confessed to not accepting or taking care of *yourself* please raise your hand? No one!

There might be a few other explanations for our difficulty with this virtue of self-love. One is that our interpretation of life's events can tend to be self-punishing. We tell ourselves that the accident was due to our stupidity, that our loneliness is caused by unattractiveness, and so on. On top of that, we have become wonderfully adept at comparing ourselves with others to measure our worth, saying "I never could do that the way he does," and thus always come out on the short end. I sometimes think if God wanted me to do it the way that person does, God would have made two of that person! Yet teens compare themselves to others when it comes to friends, clothes, grades, hair, and complexion and suffer a lot from it. The elderly can tend to rate their worth by what they *can't* do anymore, instead of who they are in the sight of God and all they love so dearly. I believe that much of the violence that grows like a cancer in the larger society is symptomatic of self-hate turned outward on others.

How can our faith in God's love, a deep, full, healing love, turn this around? One way is to view prayer as time in the company of one who longs for *ours*! (We *are* the apple of God's eye!) Another is to change a negative examination of the day ("How did I sin today?") into an appreciative "How, with the help of God, was I loving?" and end with praise, not contempt! We can also befriend ourselves the same way we would anyone we love: with time, communication, and appreciation of our unique gifts. This can usually change our thinking from "I messed up again" to "I am not all I could be, but I am a good person to be around!" A recent twist I gave to a negative thought went like this:

> A parishioner approached me with what she said another parishioner thought: that I should lock all my car doors and never park on the church lot on the weeknights I am here late. On hearing that, I spontaneously thought, "They think of me as a child! Will I never grow up?" But I quickly changed my interpretation to, "It's nice she's so interested in my safety!" This was loving to both the parishioner and myself!

Another good means toward self-esteem is learning to laugh at ourselves. Just last week, I locked my keys in the car and got lost on the same day! Being able to laugh at these—even if not right away!—gave me and others a brighter day!

One final approach to self-love is accepting compliments. An elderly woman in the parish has been consistently encouraging me because she knows I am very afraid to lead the singing in church. Recently I goofed and we both knew it. So that day she said, "You really look nice tonight!"

In conclusion, Jesus tells us today that the only thing that matters is a life lived in love. We've all known the pain of "thinking the world of people" who think little of themselves. Sometimes I imagine God weeping when watching us value ourselves so little! Today when we profess "I shall be healed" before feasting on the Body and Blood of Christ, let's pray that our wounded self-love find its cure in the love Jesus wants to offer!

6.

Trinity, Kisses, and Dancing: You Can't Do Them Alone!

Matthew 28:16-20

Over the years, teachers and preachers have used many images to describe the life of *Trinity*. The triangle, one of the most common, had three equal sides but falls short because of its inertness and rigidity. Also, the modern connotation of the "love triangle" that fills the plots of soap operas causes much pain in real life. The shamrock, while showing color and life, is far from a worthy expression of God's life. Three linked circles convey unity but no breadth. All fail to adequately illustrate the *shared life of God*.

Recently I came upon two images that come closer to what that life must be like. One is the teaching of St. Bernard of Clairvaux, who used the "Kiss Theory" to explain Trinity. His instruction is that God is the kisser; Jesus, the beloved kissed; and the Spirit the very kiss of God! I have shared that view several times in adult formation settings, and it is both attractive and fun to ponder!

The second image is that of dance, one teeming with a sort of radical optimism! God, it claims, is in the world as a dancer is in the dance. Or, to describe the unity of three Persons, the Dance is the Dancer Dancing. God here is movement, beauty, and Person fulfilling an exciting destiny!

The reason I believe those last two images are the best yet is that they are *interpersonal*. And Trinity implies that God is revealed in *relationship*. But what is going on in this commu-

19

nity of God-persons? And to what does the doctrine challenge us?

If Trinity is God-in-community, then the Persons are loving and receiving love—unconditional, inclusive, and eternal—and all those baptized "in the name of the Father, Son, and Holy Spirit" are invited into that dynamic!

The Trinity is like a group of friends who will attend a wedding of a man and woman they *all* love and decide to go together on the gift. They each could give their own but instead contribute generously and uniquely to one large gesture, three expressions in one.

The God-in-community is not an absentee landlord, a hide-and-seek mystery in the sky, aloof observer of human folly. Rather, this Trinity is a Lover who communicates, a Friend who saves, a Parent who can be counted on night or day. In Trinity, three is not a crowd; three's *company,* company we can keep!

When I taught high school English in a former life, I would always save the love poetry unit for springtime, when only such a topic could keep the seniors' attention before the excitement of graduation. I taught a sonnet by Elizabeth Barrett Browning, and I think with a slight change, it communicates what the Trinity wants us to hear today:

> How do We love thee? Let Us count the ways!
> We love thee to the depth and breadth and height
>   our soul can reach.
> We love thee freely, purely, with passion and faith.
> And We will love thee better after death.

How does one who's included in that promise respond? How do we, baptized into Trinitarian life, witness to that fact? Like heirs of any loving union, we resemble the life we share when we reflect its originator's qualities. For instance, you meet my deceased Dad when you experience dry humor, compassionate eyes, or fast driving with me! Those who've known us both can't see me without thinking of him, and the same can be said about Mom in me.

So too with our baptism into Trinity. A baptismal certificate may be the legal proof, but less convincing than when we show mutual care, lovingly include those on the sidelines, and ever extend the circle of those touched by God's love . . . through us.

Now creating that kind of community is messy and takes effort. But the Trinity is our best model, and so are those we worship and serve with who are acting like heirs of the love that God is: parents with their adopted infant, a wife and daughter with their husband/father in the hospital room, three friends energetically conversing around a restaurant table, happy to see each other and feeling closer as they share, a parish committee of three who show concern for the common good as they plan events with the handicapped in mind. Each of these models teaches us that you can't live in Trinitarian love and ignore the *human* community. In fact, our privilege as heirs of God, and our challenge as baptized, is to resist the great American temptation of rugged individualism and model community to the point where we can sincerely look at others and say, "You truly are bone of my bone and flesh of my flesh." It will be a resounding echo of our familiar prayer to the Trinity:

> *Glory* be to the Father, and to the Son,
> and to the Holy Spirit, as it was in the
> beginning, is now, and ever shall be,
> world without end. Amen!

7.

Marrieds: Don't Settle for Drinking Water if Wine Will Keep the Party Going!

Isaiah 62:1-5
John 2:1-12

Think for a moment of the highlights of your life, the grand and glowing moments. . . . Though getting a driver's license, paying off the mortgage, or passing your first algebra test may have crossed your mind, I believe most of us thought of an event connected to someone we love or one who loves us. That person made the water of routine into the *wine* of adventure. That person brought joy, even during the post-Christmas blahs or the February blues.

Today's readings are about how people turn our water into wine. In Isaiah, God says to us, "You aren't despised! You delight me! You are the joy of my heart!" Now for those of us cherished like that, nothing can be ordinary again!

In the Gospel, the dilemma of no more wine finds the fun stopping and guests gazing into the bottoms of their empty glasses. Jesus does more than miracles for them. According to anything we can estimate, He made 180 gallons of wine available to save the newlyweds from embarrassment and keep the party going. He gives us a theology of marriage and a guide for relationships in that gesture.

I read recently that most people enjoy weddings, but fewer and fewer enjoy the state of matrimony after the reception! I also read that lots of people today are washed in the waters of baptism, but few choose to drink the wine of renewed love in marriage.

For many, the experience of married love can resemble the wine at the wedding feast in Cana: It runs out! This looks like loss of interest in the partner, less patience, decreased time together, or no longer working at making the relationship happy and new each day. Sometimes, to complicate this, we run out of money or work as well. The wine of "I find you attractive; I want to be with you" can either go the route of "I'm so lucky to have a lifetime to get to know you better" or "I know you well enough to start taking you for granted." (The first is accompanied by a twinkle in the eyes, the second, by a long yawn!)

Recently, I spoke with two couples, each of which represents one of these types of marriage relationships. The first was a couple who told me when I called that they had just come inside after having a snowball fight! The other, married less than one year, could not think of one thing about each other that had initially attracted them to their spouse! I found that unspeakably sad.

I feel one of you very marrieds should be giving this homily, so I observed a Catholic couple married 21 years who gave me this next piece! They obviously have plenty of wine left in their relationship, despite illness. They tried not to interrupt each other as they conversed and complimented each other frequently. They share daily prayer together and the day I joined them for that, I discovered they thank God for each other as part of it!

I also encountered a college couple lately. The young woman went to New Jersey to meet her fiance's family, and when she was there, her future husband walked into the room while she was praying. He asked what she was doing, and they ended up continuing together. They decided they'll need to do that many times again, especially after the kids come along!

As you can imagine, neither couple I just described have settled for drinking water alone in their relationship! They're serving up *wine*! Now whenever marrieds get tired of each other, they're forgetting that Jesus was the Guest at their wedding who showed them how to keep the jars filled to the brim. So if any limits are set in celebrating continued married love, it isn't any fault of God's!

Recently, I spoke to a couple married twelve years and now separated. The husband admits to involvement with drugs and another woman, while the wife says, "Come home. I can forgive, and we'll work this out." Now he's settling for water because he isn't ready to accept forgiveness. What usually insures renewal is the new batch of wine that comes with talking the rough edges out, articulating our expectations and heartaches, or going on a date after 28 years and three and a half months!

Usually in the talking, the first sentence is the hardest, like: "I feel uncomfortable when you spend so much money on hobbies that don't include the family," or "We seem to be able to accept the fact that each of the kids is different, but translate *our* differences as faults!" or "Why can't we ever disagree without yelling?" or "Let's take a walk and talk this out!" or "I'm starting to miss you; I'm not sure I can live with this work schedule anymore!"

Jesus never said, "Settle for drinking water and let the party end!" He is the Guest who provides jars of love that last for a lifetime! Let's pray that all the very marrieds will keep the party going, and let's support everyone who's committed to the process!

8.

Mountain Streams and Married Love: A Wedding Homily

Genesis 2:18-24
Romans 12:9-13
John 15:9-11

Suzanne and Ruben,

A few hours ago I returned from a week-long back-packing retreat in the Great Smoky Mountains of North Carolina. While there, I thought of you and this event each day, and some images that are fresh from that seem fitting to share.

Being surrounded by vast, gigantic mountains was thrilling, filled me with awe, and sometimes moved me to tears! I felt embraced by something so much larger than myself, yet somehow I felt part of it. The mountains for me were the abundant love of God, and as I became filled with it, there was such a run-off, such an overflow!

Those mountains reminded me of your love: originating in the love of God, deep and broad, awesome to witness, overflowing to Abe and Jacob, extending to our parish youth, your Moms and many friends! Now that's a vast love! People touched by it are thrilled, filled, and awestruck by how far-reaching it is. And we feel not small and insignificant but infinitely more significant when we are in its presence! Thank you!

The mountain streams also reminded me of you two. I kept wondering where all that water was coming from. How could that powerful stream keep flowing, all day, every day? It was constant, faithful, and fresh. I watched it inch past all the logs and stones to create here a trickle, there a falls. Nothing could stop the flow!

It was like the life-long love you pledge in our presence tonight. It resembled for me the endless conversations you have about everything imaginable: when you plan, re-hash, solve, and question your days, your lives, your work in front of that fireplace. It was like the way you think of each other so steadily. Just a few weeks ago when I tried to learn trout-fishing with you and Abe, Ruben, as we headed for yet another bridge in Clare County, you typically remarked, "Now Sue is doing the gardening . . ." And when we arrived back, she was right there, radiantly happy!

In that steady stream, all sorts of "stuff" gets in the way of the water's flow, or tries to. Things like fallen tree limbs and large stones find their way right into the middle, but their presence is what makes the sound so powerful! They have to be gone over, or gotten around! For you, these might represent different styles. For one of you the diet works, while the other one struggles! Ruben wears the hat of the visionary, Sue the detail person. But you are both acting out of your hearts. One of you needs space on a Saturday in February, the other togetherness. These differences are but stones in the stream, and while they may bring frustration at times, they bring conversation, quiet, and finally laughter and a deeper love: the returning sound of water rushing again over the rocks!

The readings you chose are reminders for you and all of us how to love better, how to love forever. Genesis says companions for life are a gift of God! Be sure to have the mutuality that goes with it! The letter to the Romans acknowledges the need we have for the other, the significant other, to complete us. And in that dynamic of authentic love, delight happens when we honor each other. I've seen this between you many times already, like when Ruben pulled off the surprise party for your fortieth, and when you found the perfect Christmas present for Ruben last year, Sue. You both took delight in honoring each other!

But there's a wider love the reading calls us to, one I have also seen you witness. It's the overflow of love into hospitality: knowing how to open your home, share others' hurts and joys, and welcome friends with broken hearts, kids with school confusion, or maybe a minister like me on a night out!

The Good News according to John is a fitting reading, too. It recalls God as source of love and invites all who live in it to a joy that will last!

Ruben and Sue, we're here because we believe your love will last forever, and with Jesus as the third partner in this union, your love is bound to grow! We'll be there for you as it does!

9.

THERE IS LOVE: MARRIAGE AS VOCATION AND MINISTRY

John 6:60-69

When I doze off at the end of a long day of active ministry, I often reflect back on the day and where I found God. And when I have been with a married couple growing in Christian love, I never have to think further: I met God, Who is love.

I have become more aware the last few years that marriage is the most sensationalized and sentimentalized, yet grossly undersold and too little supported vocation in the Church. Perhaps the late Erma Bombeck's portrayal of family life is more accurate than the "Cosby Show" portrayal. After all, not all problems can be worked out by lawyer Mom and doctor Dad on the couch just when and how they need to be!

I would like to reflect with you on the gift and challenge of Christian marriage in light of today's Gospel theme, "It is the Spirit that gives life."

Most young marriages—even good Christian ones—thrive initially on high emotional excitement and larger-than-life dreams. And this is wonderful and very energizing. But few marriages last that don't put flesh at the service of spirit and spirit at the disposal of body in such a way that the relationship becomes a deep friendship with Jesus as third Partner and constant Guest.

Marriage to me is a miracle of merged histories, a sacrament signifying God's desire to become one with us so we can become united to another. It is God's invitation to intimacy and people's finest introduction to God as *fullness of love*.

The Church's understanding of marriage has evolved over the years. In 1964, the Second Vatican Council, in its document "The Church in the Modern World," described marriage as "an intimate partnership of life and love." Previously in the Church, clergy and religious were often thought to have a corner on holiness and salvation with their "higher callings." But with this description, marriage as vocation and ministry is seen as an equal means not only to personal holiness but also to full health and salvation for the Christian community and human family. Now women and men married in Christ could bring society *home* to full life and love: a lofty call indeed!

Church (Canon) law also re-defined marriage in its 1983 Code. Readiness to enter marriage required a willingness to enter into a partnership emotionally, psychically, and physically, that is, to invest one's entire personhood into knowing and loving another with all the thoughts, decisions, feelings, dreams, and disappointments, as well as hurts and forgiveness, that would entail. Gone was the hierarchy of sexes; mutuality and new layers of trust were called for as even the secrets of the heart were to be placed at the disposal of the other in what the Church referred to as *full communion of life*.

People might rightly ask in fear, "Will I lose myself in this venture of communion?" And the Church would assure that giving oneself only makes one more and more *married*, and losing in communion with one's spouse is the gain beyond all telling for those who risk. This is aptly described in "The Wedding Song" as the union of spirits that cause God to remain, for there is love.

Now matrimony is an event. But marriage is a process for a lifetime. You marry each other each day. Last week I was on a canoe trip with our youth and paddled down the Chippewa River with a youth minister married 34 years. I told her I liked the places on the river route where you can't tell which way it will turn. She said that was like her marriage. It seemed that every day she learned something new about this man with whom she had lived for so long.

Love grows. Couples need to grow *together*. How does it look, this spirit of God's love in marriage, this union of two whole persons on the day-to-day? I think you see it when couples affirm, not flatter, each other when conversing with other people. They're genuinely proud of each other and cherish not only the appearance and talents of the other but their spouse's personhood as well. They celebrate their differences, their unique blend of gifts, as they make their way to the goal of their covenant: unity. This process is described on the matchbook cover Tom and Jenny had printed for their April wedding here: "And there shall be such oneness that when one cries, the other tastes salt." There is wisdom in the word shall, for all very marrieds work at this and play at this for a lifetime!

How does this oneness of the whole persons of couples look? I meet it in couples married ten to twenty years. When I phone to draft them for some parish project, the spouse says, "I'll check with Tony or Debbie." Then I know that compromise merges their wills, that sacrifice and give-and-take enter their decision-making.

Recently I collected stories from couples married forty years. One woman told me she and her husband send taped letters to their grandson at college so they'll know each other when they next meet. How wonderful it was to hear that they learn about each other as they listen to the segment each records! I was with another couple at a restaurant lately, and even the way they disagreed revealed utter respect for where the other was coming from. They listened and knew where the other stood but felt no need to see things the same way. I went to another couple's home where, after the traditional meal prayer, they shared prayer from their hearts. They knew each other's greatest concerns.

I had a real treat visiting a home-bound parishioner and her more able husband. Noticing a vase of fresh, proud gladiolas on the table, I wondered out loud what the occasion might be.

She said, "He knows I love flowers. He brings them home all the time!" They have been married 65 years! They are good witnesses to the spirit of loyalty and affection that can permeate and animate a relationship even after the bodies have pretty well given out. They will love each other beyond the grave!

We have also known that relationships can die. We've seen the lights go out in people's eyes when their union hasn't been nurtured spiritually and physically. Ideals give way to cynicism, and sometimes couples stop trying. There are signs of this. I find typically he says, "She sulks and won't tell me what's wrong." She says, "I never know what he's thinking anymore." And the full communion of life begins to break down with silence, isolation, laziness, and grudges. They may stop praying alone and together or feel it's too late to salvage the relationship. Often one partner wants desperately to grow but the other is closed and afraid.

In some of these cases, the only moral, mature, and life-giving solution is to sever the tie so that quality of life can be restored to *all* family members. This is how some "for better rather than for worse" relationships must be resolved. Destructive, harmful behavior sometimes requires one to break what is no longer a loving union. The Church is slowly beginning to understand this as we witness broken lives, but there is need for deeper compassion and companioning as we welcome and support single parents and our divorced sisters and brothers with sincere warmth and comfort.

As we continue this celebration, we renew our sacramental covenant with God in Jesus, flesh of our flesh, and we taste the gift of intimacy in bread and wine shared. We say to each other with St. Augustine:

> Take, then, and eat the Body of Christ, for by the Body of Christ you are already members of Christ. Take also and drink the Blood of Christ. Lest there be divisions among you, eat what binds you together. . . . We are joined together because we share our life together.

Covenant, unity, intimacy! Amen! Come, Lord Jesus!

10.

Forfeiting All Else for Love: A Wedding Homily

Matthew 13:44-46

How often we speak of *priorities* today! Yet how few people are ever faced with having to choose at a moment's notice to keep what is of greatest value and leave the rest behind!

I had an opportunity in the late '70s while living in a frame house in the inner city of Milwaukee. In the middle of the night, our next door neighbor had a fire. As the firefighters doused his home with heavy water pressure, and as the heat intensified, our windows started breaking and we had to evacuate. I had but a few moments to awaken and choose what I would keep from all I would have to leave. That early morning, I found out what I really valued and what did not matter as I carried out to the street only the *treasures*.

When people make decisions like choosing a marriage partner, they go through a similar but more lengthy reflection on which pearl to keep, which treasure to exchange everything for and give everything to. This involves putting perfectly good opportunities aside and letting go of other possible relationships as they narrow the options. And for people of faith, for disciples of Jesus, this process of heart-and-soul-searching includes wondering about how God is active in all this:

Is the love of my life also in love with God?
Will this love of my life let God be our third Partner?
If we promise to share everything, won't we also
share the God to Whom we are committed?

32

I had an opportunity ten days ago to meet with Colleen and Mike about their wedding. What began as a brief conversation ended as a longer, more penetrating discussion about priorities, about the communion of persons, about integrity and trust and being certain of those in another. That night, I learned something about the pearl of great price they are buying in the sacramental covenant they make in our presence today.

For Mike and Colleen, knowledge bred love, and love is transforming their lives. They have valued one another since their youth, when they admired each other's skills in student council settings in Bay City. They considered each other "buddies" then, and were looking at each other as one would view a pearl through a store window, seeing its beauty without really handling it.

During their adult years, they drifted and floated awhile, with Mike sending Colleen postcards, but neither realizing as yet the treasure still hidden in the field. So for a time, neither looked for it. Until, as Mike put it, "Something moved her to call me when we were both bummed." And that call was so important an initiative, he remembers the date: October 27, 1990. He said, "We rented a comedy on video and it was like we were two old friends but strangers."

And that's how the reign of God works. Our options focus, our plans are turned upside down, our expectations change . . . all in a marvelous, only-God-could-pull-this-off way! On their second date, they spoke of religion, which was important to both of them, and by the third, children! They realized, as the writer of Matthew teaches in today's parable, that to risk all is to gain all.

Parallel to their long talks, they both invested themselves in the renewal of their spirits through the RCIA process here in 1991. Everyone could see they loved God in and through each other! It was just a matter of *when*, we all felt. Their involvement led to Mike's becoming Catholic and Colleen's completion of sacramental initiation. Ever since that Easter, they both have shared their love through participation in parish liturgical and out-reach ministries. After all, when one finds a pearl of great price, one must share the *joy* of the find.

Now when Mike and Colleen were choosing a date for their marriage, weather and time of year were not the only concerns. They consulted the lectionary to find readings that conveyed their values. The Gospel image of the pearl of great price captured the full-hearted response they vow to express they have been blessed with the love of a lifetime. It touched me to hear Mike say he had the hours counted until their wedding. It thrilled me to know Colleen and Mike had agreed that the parish weekend liturgy was the place and time for their celebration to be most meaningful. Certainly the witness of married love remains one of the greatest signs of God's action in the world.

We pray, Colleen and Mike, that this witness will grow in your lives even after diapers, mid-life, age spots, and grandkids! So lean on God, love each other well, and count on this Christian community, and your love will never grow old or cold!

In conclusion, I share a poem about the kind of friendship you seal in sacrament today:

Bethink thee, how out of . . . acquaintance,
friendship unveil'd itself in our bosoms. . . .
Yes, and rejoice in the present day! For
love that is holy seeketh the noblest fruits!
That where thoughts are the same, where opinions agree,
the pair may . . . lovingly blend into one.
(J.W. Goethe, "The Metamorphosis of Plants")

COME   COME

AND **THIS** EAT

(BLACK SHEEP)

LAMB OF

FROM WHOM

GOD

NOTHING CAN SNATCH US

PLAYFUL IMAGES WITH SERIOUS MESSAGES

1.

Potted Plants, Pecan Trees, and Good Marriages: More than Letting Nature Take Its Course

Mark 10:2-16

Recently, my largest potted plant got too out of hand and I separated it into two pots. The old root was no longer giving it enough room to grow and eventually sapped the life out of the stem. Its full potential was wasted.

After re-potting it, I found I had to change some furniture around to accommodate the two smaller plants and give them both sufficient light. It took some doing, and I hadn't anticipated the scope of the project until I was into it, dirt under the fingernails and sleeves rolled up to the elbows!

Now all of what is true about plant growth is true of our relationships in friendship and marriage. We need to provide the conditions for development, and each relationship produces change in our life.

What we want to be like is God, and God is relational. So we could say that holiness is unity, that virtue is love. But what we often experience is loneliness. The media keeps us abreast of the loneliness even of the rich and famous. They can travel, but they need roots, too. Their names are known, but they need to be accepted just as they are.

We seek to relieve our loneliness in companionship. But in so many instances, the joy and satisfaction of even that can sour into loneliness of another kind: misunderstandings about money or in-laws, failure to communicate real feelings, the boredom of routine and taking the other for granted. Still, we continue to use the external symbols of meals together, gift-giving, chores around the house, even sexual union, but forget their meaning and intent.

Why does this stifled growth happen? Perhaps because we expect one person to satisfy all our emotional and social needs and we eat each other alive. No longer is the extended family assembled; Grandpa or an aunt isn't there to take the strain off a married couple's responsibilities. Perhaps because some marry to find themselves instead of to share themselves as they continue the life-long process of becoming more loving persons.

Recently I noticed that a large branch on a pecan tree was sagging from the weight of nuts and suggested to a parishioner that he *brace* it so as not to lose the *fruit*. He said, "Why not let nature take its course? It'll cost me $9 for a beam to support it!" I listened, and today I heard a crash as the overloaded branch cracked and fell. The nuts are lost. Continued growth is impossible.

Relationships need braces, too, from time to time. Like more time to talk honestly. Like space when the roots are getting too tangled. Like the light of humor, the water of affection.

Relationships need to grow. And those who have experienced the pain of broken promises and the shattered dreams of death, divorce and rejection need compassion and time to heal. Those who are struggling need reassurance and our support. But it's those who are afraid to risk loving *at all* who will never be signs of the kingdom, signs of God's love which is faithful and endures to the end!

2.

School Crossing Guards: Intimacy with the Good Shepherd

John 10:11-18

I was moved recently to hear that one of our fifth graders raised a very significant question in class, and was glad that I could later be one who grappled with him over it. Matt said, "I don't know if I love God." His teacher was a little alarmed and asked, "What makes you say that?" Matt answered, "I don't really know if I *know* God!" That is profound because anyone who asks or wonders is on the way to knowing!

Shortly after hearing about that exchange, I was approached at the potluck by a retired parishioner who looked a little worried. She confided, "I have holes in my faith. Can we talk sometime?" Both of these questions are greatly important, and today's Gospel has something to say to each.

The Good Shepherd invites us to *intimacy*, to knowing and being known. Jesus implies here that all He and God share is available to His followers. And we know by experience that the journey of faith means entering more and more deeply into that intimacy.

Now we Americans tend to trust leaders to the degree that they know what we're going through. We don't want them to be too removed from our problems. We rely on the experience of those who have "encountered the wolf" as we have! And here we have a Shepherd who knew how to be a lamb, to the point of slaughter, choosing to be slain out of lavish love! What greater credibility could a leader have? What stronger demonstration of love?

I picture a modern and very daily image to help me understand this: a school crossing guard. In all weather, this person is a trusted companion, implicitly dependable. When the children have something to share, the guard is acknowledged, yet when they're tired or preoccupied, he or she may not be noticed. But it is this trusted adult who walks to the other side with the children, who leads to safety and would rather be injured than have one of them be touched.

Really good crossing guards do more than protect. They listen, love, advise, and settle things even as they accompany. They know each child by name, and it is *love,* not mere responsibility, that motivates their service.

So how does this kind of knowing and being known look when it comes to flock and Shepherd? I'd like to answer using the Gallup Poll, our fifth grader Matt, and a story I read once.

In 1990, George Gallup asked a sampling of people what they believed the greatest authority on *truth* was. Only 3% answered it was found in what religious leaders say. But 43% said that personal experience tells them—that *knowing* is not being told. It's going through something.

Then I asked the fifth graders, "What difference does it make that you believe in God, in Jesus and His resurrection?" One answer I received was "Because I can trust!" These children, you see, left their heads, left the pat answers, and applied my question to the dynamic of relationship!

A story from Alice Walker called "The Welcome Table" illustrates knowing and being known in this way: An African American woman gets all gussied up on a Sunday and tries to enter a White church. She's thrown out even as the Word is proclaiming God's inclusive love! Just then she looks up and sees one she thinks is Jesus walking along, but she's not sure because there's no *lamb* with Him! She becomes certain when He walks alongside her . . . like a crossing guard and a friend. This was not a hide-and-seek God. This was the Companion who loved her. Whereas the *flock* had not resembled this Shepherd, He knew the sheep and walked with them.

What's in this for us? Maybe the truth that intimacy with the Shepherd has everything to do with the flock learning how to love like the Shepherd . . . the sheep being as inclusive as the Shepherd. This might mean accompanying the stranger or sharing the road in a thousand other ways. That is what the fifth graders knew and what Jesus models.

This business of sheep and Shepherd is much less sentimental and saccharine, but much more deeply satisfying and challenging, far more nurturing and real, when we realize that Jesus is saying, "Love Me? Love My flock. Know Me? Know My flock. There are no insiders and outsiders when My flock resembles Me. I have led you all to water out of love. I have bound your wounds, kept you from the wolves of distrust. Now lay down your lives and there will be only one flock!"

The power of Jesus' resurrection can do this! Amen.

3.

Getting Out of the High Chair and Taking Your Place at Table: A First Eucharist Homily for Children (And the Rest of Us)

Mark 14:12-16, 22-26

You must feel very excited and happy today! You have waited so long for this, and we are very proud of you! Today I'd like to talk to you about what is happening so that years from now, when you are grown and far from this day, you will remember how special it was, and still can be, every time you receive Jesus. Do you remember that when you were a little girl or boy, you sat in a high chair away from the big table?

Do you remember people giving you soft foods, or smiling when you banged your little silver spoon on the metal table? Do you remember spilling your milk or dropping some of the mashed fruit on the kitchen floor?

Well, one day your folks decided it was time for you to join the big people at the table, and that was a special move for you. *today*, in our little church we invite you to the table with the big people. When you were baptized, someone carried you into the church and spoke promises for you, accepted a candle and certificate for you, and stood up to introduce you as a new Christian to the Catholic family. But today you are old enough to walk in here and say your own strong *Amen* when this community shares the Body and Blood of our Leader Jesus with you. And you will be welcome at this table of friendship with

Him every day of your life from now on. This is why we taught you the song "We Come to Your Table" for today's celebration!

Jesus wants you to come to Him, to be closer to Him than ever before! Remember the night a few weeks ago when I came to your grandparents' house, Sarah, and talked with you and Mom and your teacher? I asked you a very important question: "How does God feel about Sarah?" And do you remember what you answered? You said, "Great!" and that showed me you are ready to receive Jesus today because you already believe He wants you to share His life through this meal. He already has a special place in your heart. Your response also showed me how much Mom and Dad have loved you and taught you about Jesus all those years.

The bread that you eat with us here isn't like any other bread. It reminds us of the manna that God gave the people in the desert when they were looking all over for something to eat. And it is a sign that God never wants us to go hungry. But it's greater than that bread. It reminds us of the time Jesus took the little amount of bread a boy had and fed the hungry crowds who came to hear Him teach. But it's greater than that bread, too. It's even more special than that homemade bread Mommy made to decorate our altar today, and it's hard to beat that!

Do you remember a time you were invited to be part of something important and you were so glad? Well, today Jesus Himself invites you to a meal that will mean receiving, sharing His own life which He made possible by loving us all the way to the cross and back.

I hope you will always come to this table out of love and joy to be close to Jesus, or, when things are hard in life, out of your need to be strong and caring like Jesus. You know that when you eat junk food or spoiled food or too much of anything, you become sick. But when you are nourished by the Body and Blood of Jesus, you grow into a follower of His who looks like Him in the way you share and care and pray and play. You really do become His hands and feet, His eyes and heart to everyone the more this food and drink become part of who *you* are!

Jesus said He wanted to be remembered by this special meal. He is closer to us than a person in a photo, closer than a voice on a tape, closer than our own favorite pet. So we must always enjoy this special food and drink, which is really Jesus' life, with respect and care.

And what does this, your church family, pray for you today? That you—and we—will become more like Jesus. Dad told you that if you eat so many pickles, you'll begin to *look* like one, maybe even *become* one! By receiving Jesus, we hope to talk and act like Him. We pray that as the parish family shares this meal week after week, we will feel closer and closer to Him!

4.

The Family Tree: An Exercise in Welcoming the Stranger

Matthew 1:18-24

A great concern of many people today is their *roots*, and a favorite interest is *the family tree*. This fascination with our ancestral connections can arise from questions of family medical history, adoption procedures, approaching marriage, alcoholic rehabilitation issues, or simple love of family. The result of studying where we've come from is often pride, deepening of the sense of belonging, and, yes, *pain*.

Organizing the family history brings up chaotic dilemmas at times. One of my aunts was gathering data for ours when she hit a snag and called me. A relative of ours had two children by a first husband, a third out of wedlock, and a fourth by the second husband from whom she is now also divorced. So how should my aunt place that third child on the tree? Well, she is named and claimed on page 4, with her now single parent affirmed, though for a moment we came to a confusing standstill.

But there is another family history we all have in common. It contains our ancestry in the faith, our Jewish roots, and is found in the Gospel of Matthew, part of which we read today. It too contains some irregularities. Take note that Joseph is listed as the husband of Mary but not the father of Jesus. *why* is shown in the passage we just heard.

Joseph, like my aunt, had a dilemma. By Jewish Law, Palestinians in the first century experienced betrothal as legally binding as matrimony, and although not housed together, the couple were bound to each other so strictly that the woman was already called "wife." If one of the engaged partners were to be found unfaithful during that period, they could be sanctioned by public divorce or even death by stoning. Deuteronomy Chapter 22 said so. (This, by the way, is not good bedtime reading!)

Finding that Mary was pregnant before they lived together must have been heart-breaking for Joseph, since he loved both Mary and the Law. His decision was fitting for the strong, silent type who also lived by faith: quietly end the relationship. This was the plan, the good intention that meant no harm, the best he could do. And just as he was weary from worry and love-sick with grief, he naps and in a dream God shares a mysterious plan in what we could call the "annunciation" of Joseph! The revelation indicates Mary has been faithful, and God's activity has caused her pregnancy. To God's and Joseph's delight, he could take her home. Now this had difficult aspects, but today we concentrate on the Good News in that situation.

So often when we move from bottom-line type of rational decision-making to discernment (Where is God in this?), we discover that God wants the same thing we do: human love, creation of family, end to heartache, and everybody's name on the family tree! The revelation here and elsewhere is: Jesus is of God and God includes people in the plan for life. Here, Joseph no doubt moved from weariness to wonder, decision to discernment, intention to response. He names and claims the Child-to-be, adopts the Wonder-Son, and hands on the lineage of David to One whose birth messed up the otherwise tidy family tree of that royal line.

Joseph took Mary home, completing the promise their betrothal had begun. Being the strong type, he went beyond legalism and custom to swing open the door of Life for Israel and the whole waiting world. God's Son would become the Black Sheep we call Lamb of God, the King that Herod wanted to kill for Whom we live.

It's all so remarkable, surprising, mysterious. But the same dynamic is repeated all the time in our day. We look and don't find; we stop looking and see. An example might help: I went to Bethlehem a few years back with nostalgia, hoping to find peace in the place where Jesus entered human history. The day I arrived, there was anything but peace. Bethlehem, now Occupied Territory, was under curfew that day. Shops were closed and streets were empty because violence had shattered the night. There was an unsettling quiet. We drove through nearly deserted streets in a car driven by a Christian Arab who placed an Arab head covering on the dash board . . . so our vehicle wouldn't be stoned, he said! I looked but did not find an atmosphere set by the Prince of Peace born there.

Instead, I returned home and found right here the gift of peace alive in those who bear Jesus' name as they make a home for the stranger. I found the peace I had sought among those who include starving Somalians on their family tree by claiming them as sister and brother. I met Jesus in those parish families who have adopted babies and single parents who are struggling to make a home for their children while the righteous sit like Herods in judgment over them. I found the peace of Bethlehem among those who transport folks from the group homes to church on Sundays, and shared it with adults who take their children along when they deliver Toys for Tots so they too can see that the family tree extends beyond blood relatives! I saw a "Holy Land" when I witnessed one parishioner spend a "shopping day" taking Laotian refugee families to the dentist.

Those who move from a rational, heartless decision to exclude people who simply "are not our problem" to discerning they *are* on our family tree have welcomed the stranger. And that, my brothers and sisters, is Good News of great joy for all the world!

5.

Terminals and Paracletes: We're No Orphans

John 14:15-21

The past ten years, I have spent a considerable amount of time in airports and at bus terminals. They are the most ecstatic and the most pathetic of places, depending on whether I am awaiting an arrival or dreading a departure! One observation I have often made at terminals is that in the last minute or two before departure, people say the most important words they want their loved ones to remember. Before that, I heard less crucial remarks like, "Don't forget to pick up the dry-cleaning" or "Make sure to get the dog his shots" or "I want to see your report card when I get back!"

But then, at the very end, comes the tenderness. Those staying might say, "Be careful; you're precious to me!" or "I'm so proud of you, son!" or "I'll miss you so much!" or "I love you and won't ever forget the time we had!" Those who are leaving might say, "I'll miss you, too" or "I'll write!" or "Don't worry! I'll be back before you know it!" or "I love you more than ever!" Right before an absence, loved ones say tender things, make promises, pledge fidelity, give assurances. And it is those words that are remembered best.

Today's Gospel passage is part of Jesus' farewell to His followers . . . not at a terminal, but at a table. The words we heard today are placed by the Gospel writer in the context of what we refer to as the "Last Supper." Here, Jesus makes promises, offers gifts, and describes what an Easter faith looks like for a church about to be born: the church we are today!

Have you ever noticed how long the Easter Season is in the liturgical year? We have fifty days to savor the gift, unravel the mystery, of Jesus' risen life and how it is experienced by those of us with *Easter faith.*

Today we are five weeks beyond Easter, and not all our flowers made it this far, but the gift of resurrection faith is as accessible and its power is as real as we reflect on Jesus' final tender and challenging words. Brendan, a five-year-old parishioner, helped me understand this Gospel. I want to tell you how in two parts.

During Lent, I enjoyed coffee and donuts at his grandparents' house after Sunday liturgy. Brendan stood on a stool at the kitchen sink while the adults talked and showed everyone how he had learned to rinse dishes. Every glass or cup he wiped off, he would turn to his grandpa and ask, "Are you proud of me, Grandpa?" And Ray always answered, "Yes, Brendan, I'm proud of you." (Then he would remind Brendan not to waste too much water in the process!) As I watched that interchange, I imagined Brendan was really asking, "Are you still with me? Are you keeping me in view as you talk?" And I watched how secure he looked each time his grandpa reassured him.

We are the church invigorated with the new life of Jesus' resurrection, and we come to hear Him give us a reassurance: "I will not leave you orphaned." We need to hear those words so much that it's as though we stand on a stool and strain our ears to be told:

> I'm still here. I'm proud of you. But don't ever waste the water, the water of your baptism, on negative attitudes, losing heart, wallowing in what may feel like abandonment! *You* are the church My blood made possible! Emmanuel was the name you called me at Christmas. Now I promise you Paraclete, Helper to stand at your side always: Friend, Counselor. And you are always as close to me as I am to God if only you invite Us in, if only you never refuse to start anew, if only you would accept new

life! You may feel alone, but in Me you could never be. I promise you this not because you're wealthy or power-ful or clever or deserving or hard-working! No, this is My gift to you!

Don't we stand on tiptoes to hear that?

But back to Brendan. He helped me understand Jesus' second promise: "You love Me when you keep My word." How can we keep the word "I'm proud of you"? How can we live the word "I won't leave you orphaned"? Brendan showed me right after Easter.

I was sitting at his family's kitchen table; he was watching cartoons. All at once he left and came back with two used toy cars. He gave them to me and said, "These are for the poor kids. Could you see that they get them?" His mother and I exchanged glances; she hadn't known he would give his toys away but was very proud. Brendan was so grounded in his parents' and grandparents' love that he instinctively shared his favorite things. He did something to enlarge the circle of care. He lived the Easter faith. He kept the word "I'm proud of you; you'll never be forgotten" by assuring somebody *else* it's true!

We are the Easter church. The kind of love we share brings joy, is open to the world, never extends only to "our kind of people." Jesus' resurrection did away with the constraints of the old order of death-dealing, barrier-creating sin. Brendan already knows that great love breeds new life, and new life enlarges the circle of God's care to those who await it, to those on tiptoe who still feel orphaned! Our faith is a process by which we can become more and more assured that God is proud of us.

We leave here now with the command to keep God's Word by creating a city of joy. This is our faith. This is our Easter challenge. Alleluia!

6.

Mother Robins and the Good Shepherd

John 10:27-30

Every fall, my roommate and I stand our picnic table on end against the house underneath the porch eaves so it won't be weather-beaten all winter. Last weekend I was thinking it'd be about time to take it down. But I noticed a large, well-built bird nest on the top rung, just outside the kitchen window. And from the looks of it, there was action inside!

So Sheila and I climbed a step ladder to peer in and found two bright blue robin eggs. Then we tiptoed back into the house and were careful all weekend not to disturb the mother, who returned to the nest whenever she wasn't collecting housing materials and food. She is so vigilant, so faithful, so courageous, so protective!

And when it turned gray and windy on Sunday, she shivered but sat. When the neighbor kids made a lot of noise, she sat. And when I carefully rolled our grill past her station, she did not budge. She wants the lives of her young to be safe and grow carefully and steadily. She never gets far away. And she never lets those eggs out of her sight. I don't believe there's a creature on earth that could snatch them away from her!

What I have described is a picture of security, serenity. And lately, *we* haven't let those eggs and that mother robin out of *our* sight. Sheila named her Mimi, and it seems we're standing at the window first thing in the morning and right after we get home. We are watching the home outside our home. We're thinking about the belonging, the faith, and the care that mother, that nest, and those eggs represent.

53

It's a life-saving communion out there. It's an intimate picture of how God loves us and shares life. It's Shepherd and sheep, grace and salvation, all over again. It's the progress of life and life-to-be . . . *if* Mimi stays with it.

This is the image spring gives. And perhaps this image is more common in our experience than that of shepherd and sheep. But the love of shepherd for sheep—the vigilance, the courage, the faithfulness, the security, the shelter, the care, the feeding and protecting—is the same. And both these groupings remind us of the unbreakable relationship between the Risen Savior and us. *All* the time. No matter *what*.

Today's Gospel is so brief but so powerful! I love the line, "No one shall snatch them out of my hands." The mother robin sees to it that the eggs are warmed and covered. Shepherds provide protection for the sheep at night. And the Good News for us today is as reassuring: *Nothing can snatch us* out of God's loving hands . . . *if* we stay close. Nothing:

Not the media. Not terrorism.
Not possessions. Not our failures.
No political party or referendum.
Not loss. Not change. Not heartache.
Not even the people who want to tell us how to be happy!
Nothing.

Now that's all very comforting. But I believe we can never leave the Gospel at that. The other part is, "This nest ain't just for *you*, sweetheart!" Somehow the Shepherd insists that sheep and goats graze together. *This* Mother Bird says, "You know, you won't really grow up to love like God unless you welcome not just robins, but sparrows, and wrens, and cardinals, and finches, and, yes, even *bluejays*!" In other words, the *love* the Shepherd offers is universal, and the Church is made up of those who choose to nest with a diverse bunch of birds, a unique mix of creatures, *all* nurtured by the *only* one who could love with equal concern for *each*.

But that's just the beginning. Then, when these baby birds, these little lambs, these new followers of Jesus, weak in the knees and frail in their song, get strong enough, *they* become those who run and fly, carrying the resemblance of the one who warmed them, the one who alone is faithful and courageous and vigilant. And that's how the story goes on.

It's all about nesting and flying . . . being fed and learning to feed. It's about following until you're strong enough to lead. It's about never straying from the voice of the one who feeds us. It's about moving from the shelter of the porch eaves close to home to the wide universe hungry for Good News. And just as nothing gets in the way of mother and babies, *nothing* can obstruct the *sharing* of Good News by those ready to fly! Nudged from the nest, *we* become the ones who warm and sacrifice . . . and sometimes bump into plate glass windows and fly through storms! But *soaring* is our call. And we are held up by the love of the Risen Jesus Who never lets us out of God's sight.

There can be no stopping us until everyone hears about that! Alleluia!

Body Language and Epiphanies (An Ecumenical Sermon for Christian Unity Sunday)

Isaiah 61:1-6
I Corinthians 12:12-21; 26-27
Luke 4:14-21

It's fascinating sometimes to listen to the exaggerated *body language* we speak. When we want to assure someone of our attention, we say, "I'm all ears!" When describing a gangly adolescent growing fast, we comment, "He's got two left feet!" or an arthritic person might say on a damp day, "I'm all thumbs today!"

Now for a moment picture these literally. All ears: not a pretty sight; in fact, ugly and grotesque! Two left feet: hard to get around! All thumbs: literally can't handle things!

We learn from examining these expressions closely that we are not meant to have all one part, repeated over and over. Thank God for variety, for diversity, for proportion, for *balance* in the body! Unity in the body requires all the parts so that every part works as it should, so that every part knows its significance. Imagine if every member of your church wanted to preach the sermon on Sunday and no one of your members was willing to order the candles or pay the electric bill or type the newsletter! The Church can only resemble the kingdom of God when all the parts are esteemed and in relationship to the others, with Christ as Head. When diversity is considered a blessing, the body is healthy.

Now let's explore how today's Scripture plays this idea out. Let's examine what blessing and prophetic challenge are given today in the Word . . . what *epiphany* lies waiting to be discovered. Let's celebrate the Word that is fulfilled now, in our midst, for the glory of God!

Our setting for the first and third readings today is the *assembly*, the *gathering* of those attuned to God's wishes for the world. We, like the ancient Jews and Jesus' synagogue audience, come together for the reason they did: to hear what wonder God is working in our midst. Isaiah and Jesus felt God's Spirit take hold of their lives, and they both became gladness for the sad, breakthrough for the stuck, reminders of God's favor, delight for those who knew misfortune, promise for those in need of freedom. In other words, the body plagued with all ears would now be able to see again! The body with a heart that was broken could love again! All this because *God intervenes*, because the Head is allowed to lead! And sometimes when this grace is turned loose, the spiritual energy surprises us! Each of us has a *salvation story* in our history, a moment when the breakthrough occurred, when a prophet of God—one full of God's Spirit—told us we were favored. And we knew then that the Scripture was fulfilled, then and there.

I'd like to share my salvation story, as I do every chance I get because it is such Good News! Six years ago I was ministering in rural Mississippi. It was February and I was burned out and despondent. I heard about a healing retreat to be held some miles away and set out on a damp Friday night for what I felt would be the solution for my sad state of mind and heart. Now it had rained several inches the days before, and the gravel road I took when I left the main highway was showing the signs. At one point I realized I must have gone too far so tried to make a U-turn on the narrow path. In the process, the front half of the car dipped into a deep, muddy ditch. No matter what I did, I could not recover it from the imbalanced perpendicular position it was in. So, alone and unsure, I dug my sneakers and a flashlight out of my luggage and started walking. It was pitch dark and I wasn't even sure which direction to go, but decided the first light I saw would be help. One car passed me during that hour, but when I waved for help, the driver waved a breezy "hello" back and kept going! Finally I saw a tiny light in the distance, off the road and coming from the window of a shack. As there were neither steps nor doorbell, I climbed onto the porch and knocked as though my life depended on it! Before long, a small, elderly African American woman held the door ajar, and when the light half-lit my frightened face, she spoke before I could explain: "*You're safe now, honey. You're safe!*"

Her name was Alberta and after some conversation and letting me use her phone, she sent her son Henry down that dark road with me again, saying his truck and chain would free my car from the muddy ditch. Since he was retarded and the truck an antique, I really doubted it yet accepted their kindness. But the rusty chain and the eager man united in a struggle with nature and easily freed the car. And on that dark road in the middle of nowhere, Henry and I embraced.

Now for the moral of my salvation story: If I had said God can only speak during the day . . . in the city . . . through Catholics . . . by White folks . . . and when I expected it, I would have missed the *epiphany* of a lifetime! But Alberta gave me joy for ashes, comfort from fear. And Henry showed me the Body of Christ is not whole until each part is recognized!

Alberta and Henry and folks like them didn't subscribe to *Time* magazine and weren't familiar with Wall Street. But they were filled with the Spirit of the Lord because nothing got in the way of God's Word in their life. And what happened that night? The kingdom of God toppled my expectations of *where salvation could be found* and *which part of the body worked!* The scroll was opened as the parts of the Body had need of each other. And Jesus' reputation spread because Good News happened. The place was as seemingly insignificant on the map as Galilee was in Jesus' time. But I met Jesus more clearly on that country road after a spring rain in Mississippi than when I visited Nazareth as a tourist some years later!

Now how does this figure into our celebration of Christian Unity Week as Courthouse Square members? Directly! When *all* parts of the body are esteemed, Christ is able to be Head, and the body is healthy. Now for Saint Paul and the Corinthians, the challenge was Greeks' and Jews' in-fighting. Our churches each know what that is like, and our efforts have been to come together so we don't fall apart! Both Christian community and healthy ecumenism demand our sharing weaknesses even as we support our strengths. Either we support and share or we don't resemble the Body that Christ heads.

Last June, the Courthouse Square ministers and their families had a picnic at my house. We laughed as the grill filled up: It was Episcopal sausage alongside Lutheran burgers. Then came Catholic buns and Baptist potato salad. But when we ate the ice cream, everyone dug into the same gallon! Since then, your pastor and we other ministers have shared events much more significant than that: new babies, spouses' job hunts, family sickness and death, moving into a new house, the heartaches of parenting alongside professional commitments. And we have often prayed together.

But our congregations have esteemed each other as parts of the Body, too: singing Christmas carols at local group homes on a cold December afternoon, sharing food with the hungry at a joint food pantry site, attending your summer Thursday worship, and planning for Good Friday, Pentecost, and ice cream social events. The only reason we can do these things is because we all drink of the same Spirit. And the deeper each group imbibes, the greater will our combined unity be! None of us goes to God alone, and if Christ is the glue, we can only give praise by our efforts, edify by coming together, celebrate diversity even as we discover all we have in common. And perhaps the dream of Jesus for God's reign will come true when the churches are first in society to give the prophetic witness that *unity is possible amidst diversity*, in fact, that *diversity is not to be tolerated but embraced*! This is what a society whose fabric is torn with division needs to see first in us.

I took some liberties with the sermon today! In Catholic circles, seven minutes is the suggested length. But the time together and the rich readings prompted this longer reflection. To conclude, I'd like to bring back the picture from Luke's Gospel: All eyes were fixed on Jesus after his sermon. Each one there was moved when he told them that those very words were being accomplished right there, right then. And today, the same is true: on Hancock Street, on a snowy January day, in a small Lutheran congregation, as you listen to a Roman Catholic Sister spin out the same dreams of Jesus that the Baptists and Episcopalians and Presbyterians are hearing about a few blocks from here, the *reign* comes. Indeed, the Spirit of the Lord is upon us, in this place, in this Word, in each believer here. And we are anointed to be gladness to the poor, to say to our neighborhood, in a thousand different ways, "You're safe now, honey; you're safe!" because *epiphanies* never stop for those with the eyes to see!

anything worthwhile takes waiting

make

room

anything worthwhile takes waiting

make

anything worthwhile takes waiting

room

anything worthwhile takes waiting

MAKE WELCOME THE STRANGER IT'S A BOY

in

anything worthwhile takes waiting

the

anything worthwhile takes waiting

inn

TRUST WHAT YOU SEE AND HEAR

DESERT LIVING

ADVENT MUSINGS

1.

Making Room in the Inn: The Great Shake-up of Advent

Matthew 24:37-44

The other night I approached a parishioner's house and it looked all ready for Christmas. But inside, I learned the real meaning of Advent: readiness and making room! It happens this couple's son is coming home, a son who had brought tears as well as pleasure to his parents. Because the family's other children will be gone over the holidays, the parents hope to give this son the center stage. The mother showed great excitement and joyful anticipation. The dad was eager but realistic about the possible pain. He promised his wife not to mention the past, to remember the forgiveness he'd extended and to live "in the now." Both of the parents were preparing, making room in their hearts, readying themselves.

The Gospel today is about getting ready for Christ's Second Coming and warns if we're not prepared, it will strike like a thief or a flood: sudden and destructive! So in a sense, this is "stir up" and "shake up" Sunday, a challenge to move from apathy and complacency and ho-hum existence to urgency and excitement, awareness and anticipation. No one knows how much time they have and no one can afford to take life for granted, this life or the next!

"Making Room in the Inn" is our Advent theme this year. This means the inn of our church, our home, our workplace, our city, and yes, our heart. There are many dimensions to this making room dynamic. In myself, I make room amidst the clutter and business to reflect more. Often the magic of Christmas lights help me with the wonder of this! If, on the other hand, I tend to be the more reflective type, maybe making room will entail moving into action on behalf of another's happiness, being with people and sharing.

Making room for the Lord has many faces as well. In the parish setting, it might mean attending Scripture study or a Reconciliation service. On a personal level, it could mean praising God for the beauty of glitter and gift wrap but not being obsessed by "I want's."

We need to make room for the neighbor this season. There are so many ways to reach out. Our diocese has provided us with Holy Childhood boxes and the Nicaragua "clean off your desk and think children" project. There are nursing homes to visit and people to support with prayer. Personally, we could break the silence with someone and see the light about ourselves. Becoming concerned is how to move out of blindness.

But Advent's sense of urgency is far from frantic, hectic, or anxious. It's more like alertness, enthusiasm, and a welcoming stance toward life. It's a re-setting of priorities in light of Jesus' coming, the arrival of the One who loves us.

Each week we pray "in joyful hope for the coming of Jesus." For what do we hope? For peace, more light, more truth, more compassion, more sharing, more kept promises, more forgiveness, more true freedom, more shelters and less missile silos . . . and *we* are the ones who can make this happen as we wait!

Like the couple who expect their son, we are both joyful and healthily fearful at the thought of Jesus' return. But like the truck driver who approached Detroit tired and hungry after being on the highway all night, we will be glad to see the billboard that reads, "From dusk comes the dawn" if only we'll make our hearts ready by *making room in the inn.*

2.

Desert: Where the Action Is!

Mark 1:1-8

Desert: An Advent image that evokes much feeling, especially after our many experiences of viewing the progress of operation Desert Storm during the Persian Gulf War. Pictures of Saudi Arabia made us aware that sand, scorpions, sun, and soldiers occupy the desert. And desert is the context for John the Baptist's preaching in today's Gospel, though the modern warfare techniques were missing in his day.

"Desert" usually connotes solitariness, time on your hands, a dry, uneventful place or time: a vacuum. And those in the desert—our American servicepeople included—just want to go home! They live more in the future—in expectation—than in enjoyment of the present.

Yet John's tone is urgent! And masses of people went out to hear what challenge and good news he spoke: the promise of a Savior, if only they would change! Ironically, the desert became a place where the *action* was! And John repeatedly said the equivalent of "You ain't seen nothin' yet!" as he urged the people to watch for their Savior.

We live in a desert. It's a place where we anticipate complete deliverance, fulfillment of our fondest hopes, and freedom from the wilderness of winter and loneliness, sickness and inferiority, fear and alienation. *We are exiles yet. We need comfort still.* We sing of this need in our Advent hymns:

Come, Lord, be with Your people.
We are like dry land, thirsting!

We mourn in lonely exile here,
Until the Son of God appear.

Now our parish family has members who have discovered that God acts even in the desert. One elderly gentleman on hemodialysis now has to be carried up and down the steps, and his daily life consists of lying on the couch all day, either getting over the exhaustion of the treatment or waiting for the next one. But his joy is in memories of ice-fishing with his sons, who now carry on the tradition, and he is grateful for the two deer the family bagged this fall! In his wilderness, he still dreams.

A group of women in the parish recently found their dear friend dead in her easy chair, and now they grieve her absence when they see her empty chair here in church and at the familiar McDonald's they so often visited with her. But they are glad she did not have to spend years in a nursing home and find other friends are showing they care. *Flowers* bloom in the desert!

Some of us find our prayer dry on winter days, our creativity waning, depression setting in. Yet spiritual writers say it is precisely during these periods that growth spurts occur that are not perceived until later. The exile isn't useless for those who believe!

Finally, all of us do lots of what seems like useless waiting. *The Washington Post* reported recently that in a person's lifetime, five years are spent waiting in lines, six months at traffic lights, and eight months reading junk mail! The solution to this reality is not to move at higher speeds but to realize that everything worth waiting for takes time: friendship, flowers, a baby's birth, and the arrival of Jesus in human history! One can't pay attention in a hurry, and one-minute parenting is seldom effective. Seeing takes time, and it is worth the time it takes to *notice*!

So we can see that "desert" does not have to mean resources are dried up, possibilities are scarce, and solitariness leads to loneliness. *God acts* in the desert.

But in our deserts, we need the voice of a prophet; we welcome a messenger who can rouse us from slumber and promise deliverance. We saw our American troops visited by generals and even their President, and those messengers had had that effect.

Some of us used to think of prophets as predictors of the future. But today we know that prophets critique the present and urge change. They nudge, and even kick when necessary! They also remind people of the vision, jolting them out of dull complacency when they need it. We have some people like this in our parish. They say, "There's something here that needs doing . . . and we need to get at it!"

Now if our friend John the Baptist were here in America today, what would he say when he found out that the average citizen over age eighteen spends twenty-seven hours a week watching television and four reading the news, but only twelve minutes reading a book? How would he critique the situation? Here's what I imagine him saying:

- You have to be *solitary* to get perspective.
- God will lead us from captivity to freedom, but we need *exile* to see the difference!
- If you want to know what *salvation* is, ask a refugee who walked to freedom in exhaustion . . . and wouldn't have wanted a chauffeur!

The world *needed* John the Baptist but needs *Jesus* even more! Happy Advent desert!

3.

Our "Prove It!" Meets Jesus' Promise

Matthew 11:2-11

"Prove It!"

This is what our children tell us when we say, "This is for
your own good!" This is what our spouse might say if our love
is only words. This is what friends could say when we claim
we think of them a lot but never write or call. And this was
what I said to the television screen the other night when a used
car salesperson said he wished me a "Merry Christmas" but
had no gleam in his eye, no smile!

"Prove It!"

In the Gospel today, John the Baptist is in jail. Imagine how
difficult that was for an outdoorsman like him! And he was
imprisoned for preaching, not for a violent crime! We're told
he had some time to think there and began wondering if his life
had been worth it. He'd been announcing Jesus' coming and
now questioned whether the message got through. So he sent
his followers to ask Jesus outright, "Are you the Messiah?"
And Jesus' answer was a question: "What does the evidence
tell you? What do you see and hear?" Then he lists the wonders
and miracles that point to the work of salvation in their midst:
There's healing of the lame, people are coming to their senses,
good news is heard as good, and people's faith is giving them
happiness! Thus, Jesus' advice to them and us is: *trust what
you see and hear!* You need no other proof! Stop being skep-
tical about Me!

And what do *we* see and hear?

- School bullies have a change of heart and stop picking on their peers.
- People are saying they're sorry.
- Prayer gives people new hope.
- People we thought were out of our lives enter again, mysteriously, gratefully.
- Thoughtfulness touches even the hardest of hearts.
- Kids realize what their parents mean to them.
- Medical help reaches a nation in desperate need of canes, antibiotics, and bandages.
- Parishioners at your church fill boxes with crayons, rulers, markers, and scissors for kids in Nicaragua.
- People stop applying the Gospel challenge to their neighbor and start realizing it is for *them*, too.

The promise of lame leaping and blind seeing and deaf hearing still holds. We all still walk around with handicaps, still yearning to be freed—of misunderstandings, abuse, the pain of separation and disappointment, the grinding hurt of cold shoulders, being ignored, not knowing how to change difficult situations. Perhaps some of us cannot even feel the love and joy this season promises, at least not right now.

And because of this already-but-not-yet status of Christ's healing of the world, we do seem to need *proof* that He came, *proof* that He cares. The baby born in a stable became the Lord who left His ministry to us. So the next time we tell the Lord we love Him, let's not be embarrassed to hear Him say, "Prove it!"

4.

Visitation as Joyful Mystery

Luke 1:39-45

Visiting has become a lost art. Good visits are about as rare today as porch swings and single-car families! Maybe we don't visit because nobody's home. You have to be *home* to receive visits; you have to be attentive to recognize them! It's fascinating that many parish ministries today involve *visiting*. We have folks practicing the art of Christian visiting to hospitals and shut-ins, infant baptism families, and those grieving. Our new Befriender ministers were required to have twenty-eight hours of training to learn how to be caring visitors who know how to listen well. Maybe the churches can become models for the rest of society of the recovered art of *visiting*!

What is so extraordinary about a good visit is the thrill of interaction, whether the relationship is new as fresh snow or familiar as well-worn slippers. Our hearts skip a little when we anticipate such visits; our hearts leap some as we exchange words and feelings, and sense deep satisfaction as we remember later. We can make or break *Christmas* by the quality of our *visits*!

The Gospels give us models for everything; today's shows us a good visit. Now no news spreads as fast as *pregnancy*! So Luke brings together two women who recognize God's activity in their pregnancies as they share them. It wasn't easy for them to have a *visit*. Mary's four-day trek to Elizabeth's house was no picnic. I saw those rocky hills myself, and Elizabeth could not have known Mary was on her way! There was no MCI, Fax, or even Sprint! Mary just set out with good news and arrived

whenever she got there! No hot meal and foot bath waiting!
But surprise made the results more exciting! Imagine their
ecstatic greeting! Then remember that Luke also mentions the
prenatal recognition of Jesus by John the Baptist in that same
scene, the greeting that led Elizabeth to speak the prophetic
"Who am I to be honored with a visit from the mother of my
Lord?" And this does not translate "Why me?" but rather,
"Isn't it wonderful I'm here, now, for this?" This was the *joyful
mystery* our rosary now recalls as *the Visitation*. But then, when
the life of God in *anyone* meets the life of God in *another*, the
visit is always a *joyful mystery*!

Advent at this parish has been one joyful mystery! Last
Sunday the Courthouse Square Churches' carolers were at the
seventh of nine group homes they planned to visit. It was cold
and getting dark. We were a motley, rather un-musical band
who couldn't even *see* our music anymore! A group of residents with Downs Syndrome came out on their porch and
screamed, "That was beautiful!" with tears in their eyes after
every verse! My heart leaped at that joyful mystery!

The next day I visited Mary, a parishioner who suffered a
cerebral aneurysm many weeks ago and has been unable to
speak since. She struggled several times to say something and
then came out with three words in a row that formed a short
sentence. It doesn't take much conversation to make a visit a
joyful mystery! My heart jumped and her brown eyes sparkled!

That same day our high schoolers heard shrieks of joy and
surprise as they shared a meal and gifts with members of a halfway house who'd known mostly harsh and painful visits the
years before! This too was an eyeball to eyeball recognition
that *Jesus* dwells in the stranger . . . a joyful mystery!

It's not an accident that the classic, original *joyful mystery*
of *visitation* was experienced by two women who were unlikely
candidates for pregnancy: one a young virgin, the other a
barren old wife. That makes pregnancy itself a joyful mystery!
I was reminded of this during the movie *Junior*. Arnold
Schwarzenegger starts out with scientific curiosity to observe

a pregnancy experiment and ends up a believer in joyful mysteries . . . mysteries like life's sacred dimensions, sensitivity to others' pain, the cost and the adventure of caring, and the blessing of *visits* with others who bear life, too. A church pregnant with Jesus' life could learn something from Arnold's joyful mystery!

I really had trouble concluding this homily because there are many more joyful mysteries happening. But one more image is my last! I live in Bridgeport, and a sign in the window next door announces "*It's a Boy!*" because our neighbors Ann and Keith just had their third child after a troubled pregnancy that took them to Flint and kept the whole neighborhood scared for them. These days lots of *visits* are being made to bring gifts to their newborn son. When I went over to hold Lance for the first time, Ann told me the thing that helped her the most through her pregnancy was getting together for *visits* with a friend who was also expecting. Their names aren't Mary and Elizabeth, but the life growing within the one encouraged the life struggling to grow in the other. Their hearts skipped when they visited!

I think we should have a sign on our church door:

"It's a boy! Born here every time we're together!"

People would want to visit, and after their hearts felt the thrill of interaction, they too would go to a lot of trouble to spread good news with the recovered art of Christian visiting because they'll know *visits are a joyful mystery*!

IT'S

DIVINE

babies change everything

(ISN'T IT?)

wrapped in the warmth of light

TO BE

star of wonder

HUMAN

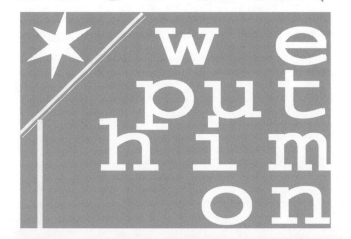

we put him on

CHRISTMAS AND OTHER SUCH GIFTS

1.

It's Divine to Be Human: Lessons from Norman Rockwell and Jesus

Luke 2:1-14

It's Christmas Eve, the night of the "Great Gift Exchange"! Our homes the next 24 hours will find floors covered with paper and ribbon, boxes and brightly-colored parcels of every shape and size. I've often found special joy in giving:
- what people have wanted for a long time
- what they needed and can't any longer get along without
- what they can use daily, and remember often of the love of the giver

These gifts are welcomed and their arrival is a cause not just for surprise, but genuine relief!

This community received a special delivery from God tonight: a Gift we've wanted a long time, need each day, can't get along without. And this Gift is a daily reminder of the goodness of the Giver! (Here, a small child unwraps a large, framed painting of Jesus as Man.) *Jesus has come home!*

(The child and the homilist carry the raised image of Jesus around the church, saying a litany of titles: "Prince of Peace," "Lamb of God," "Good Shepherd," "Messiah Long-Awaited," "Savior of the World," etc. They conclude with *"God Has Visited the People!"*)

Now, what difference does it make that God delivered this Gift of Jesus for the life of the world? The difference is that because Jesus came to express God-with-us, *it's now divine to be human!* Let's unwrap that gift a little.

75

Recently I visited the new Norman Rockwell Museum in Stockbridge, Massachusetts. There, I realized what is so attractive about Rockwell's portraits: He saw the best in human nature and the extraordinary in the ordinary. There was absolutely nothing disgusting, degrading, or negative in his images of humanity. In fact, the viewer was treated to the wholesome side of people, seen in the best light as free, good, amusing, and generous. Rockwell, in my estimation, perceives human nature like God does: *It's divine to be human*! Peace, hope, and joy are possible! And we exchange gifts because we see that potential in each other and want to nurture it.

I was so taken with Rockwell's collected works that I wanted to find out where he drew his subjects from. I learned that he and his wife bicycled through the streets of their little New England village each morning, just observing the common folk getting ready for the day: walking to school, opening the shops, carrying groceries home, and starting an ordinary day. Then, in the afternoon, Rockwell recalled the faces, the postures, the expressions, and transferred them in his inimitable way onto canvas.

I was so impressed by this that I went into the village later that day myself, and tried to look at each person on the sidewalk as a potential subject: "Will you, news carrier, be in the gallery? Will you, girl with her dog, find yourself on a canvas? Will you, retired couple enjoying the late afternoon sunset, be immortalized by one who sees your heart?" And all of a sudden I realized that every person in that village looked good and beautiful because I saw them as Rockwell had!

Now we all know that not everyone would subscribe to this outlook; nor did they subscribe to the *Saturday Evening Post*! Of course, not everyone bought into God's version of a Savior in the person of Jesus either. Besides, for lots of people in misery, it's often *not* so divine to be human because, at least at the moment, the consolation of salvation and the dignity of the incarnation are not felt! I guess this means that the people wrapped in the warmth of light need to share it, that is, the people who use the name Christian because they follow the one who shows us how divine it can be to be human.

Christmas, finally, carries much nostalgia. I for one remember a custom we had in our family. Dad opened the same gag gift, wrapped differently, each Christmas Eve. It contained a tacky bow tie and gaudy socks. It was a gift re-presented but never worn!

But not so with this Gift of Jesus. He comes to abide, to live with us. We put Him on, wear His values, bear His attitudes. And when we do this, the Great Gift Exchange is complete. It is then that the world knows it *can* be Christmas every day because *it's divine to be human*!

2.

Meeting Ourselves Coming and Going: Herod, Astrologers, Gifts, and Stars

Matthew 2:1-12

We can meet ourselves coming and going in today's Gospel. We are the Herods and the kings. We are the gifts and the star.

Herod

Now there was a clever politician, a fierce ruler! But when Jesus was born, he turned into a frightened king. He had, after all, riches, a title, and power to protect. He had assassination or usurpation of the throne to fear. He was locked into his own self-interest, and so intimidated by Jesus' appearance that he used the only tactics he had learned: He considered the stranger an opponent and planned a conspiracy in case His presence would get in the way! So he sent spies to check out the situation and began putting pins on the map. He wanted nothing new under the sun to disrupt his kingship. His motto toward the idea of accepting the Messiah was "No Way," and we might picture him with clenched teeth: a loner, paranoid, a leader with little hope and nothing to expect or believe in.

Sometimes *our* fears can act like that.

Astrologers

But we are also like the astrologers: passionate about following and eager to share gifts. We are open and happy, receptive and willing to journey far for the truth, especially when we sense we are moving toward that Someone we believe in. In the pursuit of that meeting, there is only one motive: love inspired by faith. We expect to find what we look for, and our vision turns to delight and wonder when we do! Faith, not intelligence, leads us. The invisible becomes somehow visible. Our motto had been "Go for it!" Our stance was alert eyes, and feet that are used to walking.

Gifts

The gifts of the Magi form our tradition of exchanging gifts at Christmas. But did the Infant *need* gold, incense, myrrh? No, but Christ's followers need to give gifts such as these. It would be like you, who work with bees and dairy products and stationery and cattle and medical supplies bringing honey, cream, greeting cards, beef, and cotton to the altar and then receiving the Eucharist in exchange. The signs of our livelihood are a delight to God, but the generosity of God can never be outdone. The gestures of offering, not the objects, come from the heart of us . . . like the tune of the Little Drummer Boy.

The astrologers gave commodities and received a Savior. We well know how babies change everything! They melt our winter crustiness and can make barriers crumble and fall. Such immense gifts humble and amaze us until we are so off-guard, we must adore, we must kneel at the feet of so great a Love.

Stars

For the last twenty years, people have spent large amounts of money for items that explained the zodiac, yet there is little real proof that the stars tell fate. On my vacation I always go where I can see them because, for me, they represent possibility, hope, and wonder.

Stars can cure the scared in us. It's just too bad that one of the strongest meanings of "star" for us today is celebrity, the person wearing glitter who stands in the spotlight but offers us little inspiration!

But the *Star of Wonder* got the astrologers moving—through rough terrain and foreign territory, possibly for as long as two months. And when the star led them to Jesus, the *Epiphany* took place: Love was manifested, hope revealed, and their hearts throbbed with joy! And those same gifts were meant for Gentile and Jew, women and men, old and young, frail and strong, black and yellow and red and white, rural and city dwellers: everyone who would search!

Now everyone who meets Jesus goes back by another route. It's just never the same again! It can't be business as usual, and the yawn of boredom is in the past. But we need to keep our eye on the star. We need to pass the baby around. The more Light we take in, the more we can radiate. And once that catches on, glitter just won't satisfy. Then, sisters and brothers, there will be no strangers, no opponents. Only long caravans of good and simple people seeking the True Light. Happy journey!

ESSENTIAL SUFFERING

interruption
or

✚ grace

with

PASSION
COMPASSION

BRING
EXPERIENCE

LIFE . . DEATH

EVIDENCE

READINESS

THE TREASURE

WORD

1.

Words! Trouble or Treasure?

I Corinthians 12:12-30
Luke 4:14-21

Last week it occurred to me again how important words are. I listened to an inaugural address hoping I could trust the words that sounded like promises. I attended a spelling bee, where one word misspelled put a youngster out of the contest. And I conducted a Scripture study class in which *The Word* of God revealed God's constant care for us. What a week of *words*!

Words are a *treasure* for us; we all have them. But rocks, trees, oceans and even mammals don't. One of the things that makes us the noblest of all creatures is precisely this gift of communicating with *words*.

But words are a mixed inheritance for humans. They can encourage or kill. They are both blessing and curse. Let's see how Jesus Himself uses words, *The* Word, in the passage from Luke today.

Here is the hometown boy returning for a visit and chosen to be a reader at the local synagogue. And the Scripture text becomes for His ministry—as well as our parish life—an inaugural, a measuring stick, a point of departure for the deepest of goals in the service of God's reign. What Jesus reads indicates that believers are called to bring and be Good News, to make their lives and their words life-giving. And how does that look when it's activated? The poor can smile, those enslaved see a way out, the dull are refreshed, and *all* find favor with God. Jesus who read this prophecy was Himself the embodiment of these lived ideals, the Teacher who lived what He taught, the one whose Word was always good.

Let's examine some of our words that are blessings. How about "thank you," "I love you," "Good to see you," "Nice job!" and "Can I help?"? These expressions unify, build up, include, invite, affirm, welcome, and connect people.

But then there are the ones that curse. Like "What'd you do *that* for?" or "I'll kill him!" or "Nigger!" or "You wouldn't want to see *my* house!" or "They're not *our* kind of people!" These words blame, divide, judge, and isolate. What a different feeling they carry than the first list!

Words can get us into trouble. Gossip, idle talk or guess-work about others' lives and motives are dangerous territory. So are words that carry empty flattery, insincere compliments with underlying expectations of pay-offs, or promises that aren't followed by action. These words often conceal rather than reveal, and thus cheapen the power of communication. They are as untrue as lies themselves. We might feel cheated by these kinds of words, for example when we hear, "I have no recollection of that conversation."

Words, in the creative plan of God, also bring life. How often my Dad's letters are full of good news. They encourage and inspire me, make me laugh and give me hope. Recently he wrote of visiting his best friend in the nursing home, and how they ate chocolate and listened to favorite songs. He mentioned the neighbor children, bird nests, recipes, and jokes. Then he sent greeting to those with whom I lived. It was a letter full of good news!

Just what must we do to have our words become Good News? First, we must learn to say what's in our hearts. How often we keep that for private thoughts! Also, we need to be so in touch with God's Word that when we speak, we are in fact communicating God's love, like when a loving husband and wife finish each other's sentences because they are so familiar with the other's thoughts and feelings! Remember the stark reminder Paul gives us in today's second reading: We are indispensable to each other! So to hurt other members hurts me and all of us. Maybe the best measure of whether our words are blessings would be for us to ask ourselves at the end of each day: Can I say what Jesus says in the Gospel today, that right now, as I speak these words, there is gladness? If so, my words are giving life to a needy world!

2.

Wouldn't It Be Wonderful If: A Look at Misery in Scripture

Job 7:1-4, 6-7
Mark 1:29-39

Wouldn't it be wonderful if:
- no one felt like Job of the first reading: so miserable, with days full of grief and nights that seemed never-ending . . . overwhelmed with a "What's the use?" attitude;
- everyone felt like people in the Gospel today, not being complete if they *don't* share with their neighbors?

Both the first and third reading today direct us to the fact of human suffering. And the onset of suffering, or for some, its constant presence in life, sometimes forces us to question God. There seems to be no answer science or reason or even a stretch of the imagination can give, and we are left with *"Why?"* Why do good people suffer? *Why* do the young die or give up? *Why* are people so cruel to each other? *Why* don't my best intentions bring results?

Christianity is distinguished from many other religions in its belief that suffering is essential and meaningful, not a sign of God's disfavor, nor a curse! It is not a punishment nor an unnatural disruption of luck. It is, rather, constitutive of human life and spiritual growth. It is a stepping stone toward holiness, not an abnormal intervention to obstruct the happiness that we so desire.

What, then, are our beliefs about suffering, and what, based on the Founder of Christianity's own participation in it, can we say is our theology of suffering? First, Jesus, Son of God, suffered. He was not exempt but is our Exemplar. When we suffer because of our discipleship or because of life's twists and turns, we identify with Him in a special way. We are reminded of this compassionating dynamic often when we see people take on situations of hardship because they want to assist another with a burden too heavy for one person to carry alone.

Another factor, and this more related to the spirituality of suffering, is that it humbles and mellows us, softens and sweetens us. When we have to give up control and ask for others' help, when we have to slow down and listen rather than rush and talk, we have to face the fact of our profound need, our precious gift of mortality, and we may even learn to pray more honestly, thank people more graciously, and hold every moment more tenderly. My own mother is a good example of this dynamic. An energetic and talented woman when younger, she became debilitated after a major heart attack. And she was never more lovable than in her weakest days, never more sensitive to human goodness and the presence of grace than when she could no longer *do*, but qualitatively *be*.

In addition, suffering helps us understand others better. Psychologists tell us that there are two experiences common to all human persons, no matter their age or culture: anxiety and depression! This unites us in ways we are sometimes unaware of in daily life. The other day I watched two men listening intently to each other's troubles in the post office. They took turns speaking, and by the looks on their faces, understood by experience the pain the other knew! Certainly the suffering of others is an opportunity for us to show care. Take the Gospel today. Jesus noticed physical need. Jesus responded. Then Jesus challenged His followers to help feed. This pattern is repeated today in a thousand forms by those of us who minister in His name.

The *sin* of this world in relation to suffering is threefold, I believe:

- cheating ourselves of the opportunity to learn from pain by denial via addiction, a numbing mechanism;
- glorifying those who never seem to experience pain, such as the rich and famous whose pain is absent from the press' focus;
- prolonging the suffering of others by selfishness and laziness on our part.

In conclusion, we see in the Gospel today a Jesus who goes from the synagogue to the sickbed, from the passion of prayer to the compassion of service. We leave here and do the same because our belief about misery is that, while it is essential to life, it is most meaningful when shared by those for whom the Eucharist exudes the power to love.

3.

Looking Out of Street-level Windows: Time as Opportunity

Mark 6:30-34

One day while teaching in the suburbs, I looked out the street-level window of the English classroom to see a man who had collapsed on the sidewalk while shoveling his snow. Already paramedics had arrived and were desperately trying to revive him. I decided to stop everything and have the students watch the valiant attempt at life-saving going on outside in the freezing temperature. This distraction provided a better lesson than reviewing a Shakespearean duel, it seemed! But we could have missed its significance if we had stuck to business as usual!

Think of how often you became diverted from your immediate goal to attend to what appeared to be a disruption in activity—and came away greatly enriched. Look at a day in your life. You're standing at the microwave trying to scratch supper together and your spouse or child drops a remark that might give a clue about their recent discouragement or moodiness. Is that a mere interruption? A waste of time? Taking you from what you really need to complete? Or is it more deserving of a response than the task at hand?

Or say you're finally settling down with the newspaper, catching a few quiet minutes for yourself after the kids are settled in for the night. And if it's not the phone, it's the next door neighbor ringing the doorbell. The party's over. Or could it be there's as much peace in the reassurance you can give as the silence you would cherish?

In the Gospel today, Jesus and His friends had just finished a tour of healing and teaching, and the crowds beat them to the deserted place they had hoped to escape to for rest and relaxation! Jesus did not treat them as a nasty interruption, an irritating annoyance. His heart felt pity because they lacked direction in life. He chose to care, and His followers learned more from His spontaneous response than a multitude of rabbinical teachings in the synagogue!

Our challenge to conversion lies in the difference between "killing time" and making the way for grace at any moment. This week we are invited to have *the time of our lives*!

4.

God? Exist? A Buried Treasure!

Matthew 13:44-52

In late June, I was driving back to Michigan from Milwaukee and stopped to buy a *Chicago Tribune*. In it I found an article that really fascinated me, one that I knew would visit a homily some weekend! It reported that there had been a Sunday night debate in South Barrington, Illinois, that was attended by over 6,000 people! The formal argument? Whether *God exists*! A famous atheist scholar and a convinced Christian each had 20 minutes to present a formal statement; then there were rebuttals, and a vote by the audience, who acted as jurors. The tally showed an overwhelming acceptance of *God*: 6,001 to 157! According to the article, most of those in attendance were already committed to Christianity or atheism, although a handful of the "spiritually confused" came as well. The reporter observed that most people in that packed auditorium listened carefully, hoping to learn something they could use to debate the subject in their own circles. Christians interviewed later said the argument exposed people to evidence that Christianity is true and that there is no evidence that atheism is!

Let's add to the information the results of a Gallup Poll done in 1990. It surveyed 2,200 adults about what the most believable authority on *truth* is. Is it the Bible, the Torah, parents, books, television, the word of religious leaders, or their own personal experience? Only 3 percent answered religious leaders, 31 percent said the Scriptures, but 43 percent responded personal experience!

Now what do these two studies have to say to us, and why do I bring these into our reflection on the Gospel about treasures and pearls of great price? Certainly most of us are not up to a formal debate about God, and if we were, we might be among the "spiritually confused"! And in a poll, we would probably choose the Bible as reliable. But the fact that personal experience is so vital to many individuals' faith in God points to the precious discovery our Gospel presents: If we are among the faith-seekers, what people will see in our lives is truly what God *is*: love, mercy, forgiveness, healing, truth. The more we reflect on our experience of these, the more valuable a treasure they become. And the more we treasure these, the more readily will we let go of personal ambition, selfish goals, old grudges, and negative judgments.

People in the Mid-East at the time of Jesus often buried treasure to protect it from intruders, but some forgot where they left it, and then it did neither them nor their enemies any good! We're here because our *experience* has led us to a precious treasure: the pearl of life with God in Jesus. If we bury that gift by carelessness, or forget where we put it by taking it for granted, the reign of God goes no further. But if we accept it and share it, the Scriptures will speak, being human will make sense, and all of life will seem touched by the sacred! Then, sisters and brothers, we can ask for miracles because we've *seen* them!

5.

The Virtue of Readiness: Keeping Our Eyes on the Prize

Luke 12:32-48

"Don't leave home without it." We've been warned of this in television ads for years. It stresses the virtue of readiness we are practicing all the time. Think of the U.S.A.'s pride in its defensive posture, with a military budget to prove it! Consider the instant popularity of I.R.A.s, assurance of financial planning with a view to readiness. Picture parents setting up the crib and mobiles in the baby's room long before Mom delivers! Notice gardeners covering flowers before the first frost, ready for a temperature change. And recall that the church now celebrates various stages of readiness with her candidates and catechumens to be initiated at Easter. Readiness is something we are used to.

What are the requirements for readiness? Alertness to what is really important: "Where your treasure is, there also is your heart." So often this prioritizing is achieved in mind games we play, like imagining a fire and deciding what one item to carry from the burning house. Or picturing ourselves about to have an automobile collision and seeing our whole life flash before us, wondering if it is in good enough order for us to be ready to meet God. Or pretending to pack for a trip but being able to carry only the three most important items.

Sometimes fear goes along with preparing. Anticipation can require real courage. Think of Anne Frank and her family during the Nazi occupation: alert and brave, fearful and ready.

I remember one woman in the hospital telling me she had been told she might lose her arm, and as she anticipated the decision, she became more alert to the value of that precious extremity!

But the Gospel says that being ready is only part of it; we must also work toward what we hope for, urgently getting our priorities in order as we do so. We know from experience that ill luck or changing circumstances can make that impossible. However, if we are preparing ourselves for the only real and lasting treasure all believers are promised, our readiness will look like this as we continue the life-long process:

- becoming more forgiving
- deepening our honesty
- praying from the heart and
- placing less value on what won't last.

Jesus' assurance "Don't be afraid" is followed by a command: sell what you have and give alms. He knew that kindness is more permanent than hoarding, that providence is more enduring than luxury. As people of faith, what keeps us alive is what we are readying ourselves for: Is it the birth of a grandchild? The first day of school? Seeing someone again? An end to pain? Heaven itself? Where our treasure is, there is our heart. We pray today to keep our heart in the right place until we see Jesus' face. And we know it's there when we are creating a heaven here on earth by the love we are willing to share!

6.

Maimed and Injured to Whole and Healed: The Reign of God

Mark 9:38-43, 45, 47-48

Now *this* is one of those Gospels it would be *dangerous* to take literally! Jesus just could not suggest decapitation, drowning, and maiming ourselves! On the other hand, it would be *disastrous* not to take this Gospel seriously! Jesus uses dramatic language and grisly images to describe what He is *dead serious* about: the reign of God and our full participation in it! So Jesus is really suggesting, "I want you whole not maimed, happy not injured. *All of you, every single one!* But first there are a few things you must agree to, with all your hearts!"

First, desire more than anything that *everyone* God made would enjoy a large portion of God's Spirit. This isn't easy. In the Gospel today, Jesus had to reinforce an investment in this among His followers. And somehow over the years, *churches* haven't been so good at keeping it in view, either, often prone to *excluding* those with a *large* portion of God's Spirit! Churches have had good intentions, like "safeguarding" the gift of salvation or keeping doctrine "pure." But in the process, we made God's Spirit a personal asset, a private possession, and corporately denied access to others!

Think of the years we Catholics publicly blamed our Jewish brothers and sisters for the death of Jesus every Good Friday. Today we're enlightened and call that anti-Semitism! Ponder on the centuries Catholics didn't set foot in churches where other followers of Jesus worship as faithfully as we do.

Today, ecumenical cooperation is a boon! Consider the times we made holiness the sole responsibility of nuns and priests, forgetting the dignity of our baptismal calling. Today, we celebrate baptism at Sunday liturgy to emphasize the *universal* call to holiness! Imagine the immense gulfs of hostility created between families and faiths because groups, all in the name of Jesus, claimed *exclusive* rights to God's Spirit, and, in the process, blocked it! We were cutting off our own arms, plucking out our own eyes, maiming the Body by not *wanting* it whole!

But Jesus knew the Spirit of God could not be rationed, and he reminded His followers to rejoice when *anyone at all* was seized by that Spirit to do good in His name. For whoever isn't against us is for us!

And the second thing Jesus seems to ask us to agree to if we are to fully experience God's reign? To rid our hearts, churches, neighborhoods, and work places of every obstacle that jeopardizes the power of Jesus to do good. That means to be disgusted by what steals people's joy and keeps them miserable. For *God's sake*, we must root these out . . . not cutting off our arms, but extending them!

Just maybe, if Jesus were addressing us today with this Gospel mandate, it would sound like this:

> Suppose your obsession with golf or shopping or video games makes you a stranger to your family. Throw away your clubs, your car keys, your purse! Better to live in good relationship now than enter Hell with an Arnold Palmer handicap or perfect wardrobe!

> or

> When alcohol, drugs, or any addiction is destroying you and making your family feel hopeless, isn't it better to get help now and experience new life than die early and drag the whole household down as well?

When Jesus says to cut off the sinful arm and gouge out the sinful eye, He is saying we can do without the sinful habits we cling to like limbs. They only get in the way of *real* life!

Today we are invited to take the power of evil seriously, root out what blocks the Spirit's impact, and leave the shackles behind. If we do, we'll roam into the expansive world of God's reign, where incredible good can be unleashed by the power of Jesus' name. *For God's sake*, let's not derail the Spirit's power, in Jesus Christ, our Lord!

7.

The End of the World: Now and Later

Mark 13:24-32

One night in September I thought I heard a description of the *end of the world* on the evening news. A nurse who was at the site of the USAir crash in Pittsburgh said of the wreckage scene: "We found no faces." It was one of the most tragic sentences I have ever heard.

We associate the end of the world with the worst thing that could happen. A lot of people spend their lives wondering when and how. And when we feel people are overreacting to a bad situation, we reassure them by saying, "Well, it's *not* the end of the world!" But all the little traumas, and many of the massive natural disasters like earthquakes and floods, are signs, are preparations, if only we'd let them change us!

The Gospel today describes the end of the world in apocalyptic terms, that is, dramatically and symbolically interpreting what is mystery for us all. The scenario is catastrophic, cosmic, and sweeping. Its urgency is meant to grab our attention. The Jesus of this Gospel is not a sweet, stained glass image of meekness, but rather a strong proclaimer that distress precedes relief in God's scheme of things!

Let's look at some of the images of the end time and how they are already experienced in small ways: right here, right now:

- "The sun will be darkened." Some people already know the absence of light in lonely lives or having the curtains fall with the sound of a terrifying prognosis.

- "The moon will not give light." Victims of "ethnic cleansing" know what darkness is: rejection, ridicule, and senseless violence.
- "Stars will fall from the sky." Our dreams can come crashing down . . . and have. Our earth weeps from abuse and neglect.
- "The powers of the heavens will be shaken." We face the sobering reality that some of what we strove for was empty, shallow ambition and has torn our relationships to shreds.

Each of these pains—a personal, family, or global calamity—seemed like the end of the world for those who experienced it, and each is fair warning that our obsessions can never replace love.

The world as we know it can and does fall apart from carelessness, illness, accident, and loss. If only we could read these calamities as signs that we need to fall into the arms of a God whose world is ordered chaos, perfect communion, and ultimate peace!

How many of us have regretted that we haven't read warning signs along the way! I still regret not realizing that my Dad's little kitchen accidents were small strokes that came right before the big one that killed him. How often spouses sense their partner's depression corroding the marriage without seeing a breakdown or the break-up of the family following close behind. Healing may not happen when we don't read the signs.

But we're not here to inflict guilt or encourage sadness. We're here to look at the big picture, the world as God knows it. This is the world Jesus describes as "God's word never passing away" no matter what, the world where love is all in all, where life as we knew it is past, and God's dominion of goodness and union replaces that old order of turmoil and isolation. This is the reign Jesus inaugurated and the one for which we are now responsible.

What signs of this reign already dawn? How is this new, this really *real* world coming to be? I saw several signs just last week:

- I met a group of people seeking spirituality, not just religion, and they described the crosses they bear because Jesus is their priority.

- I realized again that some of the poorest nations of the world are giving the universe its best "soul" food by creating brilliant music and art.

- I saw minorities formerly banned from voting turn out in great numbers at the polls.

- I witnessed the church's laity taking their rightful place in the church formerly closed to their gifts because of elitist structures.

- I see the world becoming smaller, the old order passing away, when I witness our youth ministering here today, and I know the hope of the world lies in their healthy participation and refusal to remain on the sidelines.

We're in the end times: the end of the church year, the end of the century and millennium. And we all like happy endings. It is Jesus, the One in Whose memory we gather, Who brings present and future together, uniting heaven with earth despite the world as we know it falling apart. Our Gospel today is meant to wake us up to realize what really matters, lasts, and counts, and to allow God to direct the events that seem so uncertain. We can trust God as we wait in joyful hope for the coming of our Savior, Jesus Christ. For people of faith, *that* is a happy ending!

A THORN IN
THE FLESH
IS A
CHRONIC
PHYSICAL
MENTAL OR
MORAL
CONDITION
-A NAG-
GING AN-
NOYANCE

TRUTH
& ~~REJECTING~~
CONSEQUENCES
THE COST OF ~~THE PROPHET~~
SPEAKING
A MOUTHFUL OF TRUTH
ARE YOU A THREAT
TO THE   EVENTUALLY THE TRUTH
             SETS US ALL FREE
COMFORT ZONE?

PROPHETIC CHALLENGES

1.

Credentials, Qualifications, and Looking Gift Horses in the Mouth

Ezekiel 2:2-5
II Corinthians 12:7-10
Mark 6:1-6

Insisting on credentials can get us into trouble. Sometimes qualifications can stymie the Spirit, can block God's work. And sometimes human nature rejects the voice of the prophet.

Look at today's three readings. First, Ezekiel the prophet claims God's Spirit gave him the courage to proclaim a message of repentance. His qualification to preach was his *experience* of God. Yet when he was sent to Israel, the people rebelled. Then Paul names his chief credential as *weakness*, a thorn in the flesh which Biblical experts say is a chronic physical, mental, or moral condition, a nagging annoyance which people knew about. But this qualification forced Paul to depend upon grace, to rely utterly on the power of Christ. And he bore insult among the Corinthians. Finally, Jesus works every sort of *wonder* and is sought after all over Palestine . . . except at home where there's no hero's welcome, only skepticism because this local son forgot His roots and now claims authority from God, no less!

These three prophets found out that if the credentials you name and claim are spiritual, if your qualification to speak is that God spoke to you, people tend to look *elsewhere* for a message. And God's Word is stymied.

How does this dynamic work in our day? Can we expect it to be easier for us than it was for Ezekiel, Paul, and Jesus? I think not. We're disciples of Jesus who take our cues for living from Him. We attempt to sign God's presence in our limited but needy world. If we would wait until everyone were convinced our actions are wise, we would seldom exercise a prophetic ministry!

When Alabama seamstress Rosa Parks took the first step in desegregating buses in the South, she seemed to have few credentials to change policy. But her simple action changed the course of history and challenged others to change their behavior. We, like her and like Jesus, need to stay with the task of letting what God tells us guide our speech and actions—and then expect a variety of consequences to result!

This is no easy task and is certainly the hardest to practice at home. *Familiarity* can breed *contempt*—and can fail to qualify in the eyes of familiar others. A prophet is less appreciated at home:

- Children, the fragile, or the otherwise least qualified often point out the truth of a situation and call us to change. But because we're unused to taking them seriously, we can miss the prophetic, and God's work can be stymied.

- Familiarity is no credential when some women and married persons in the household of the Catholic Church, their own dear faith family, claim a call from God to serve their faith family as priest, and leaders squelch even the discussion because qualifications were set long ago as gender and tradition. And some who feel belittled and ignored leave the household, knowing well what it costs to be a prophet in one's very own country.

- Oscar Schindler of *Schindler's List* was a wealthy member of the Nazi Party living a self-absorbed life. One would hardly look in his corner to find a prophet! His flaws were too well-known, his sins public. But the suffering he saw changed him, and he risked life and prosperity for Jews, speaking a truth both unpopular and dangerous . . . and finally became a hunted man.

None of these prophets could predict or control the effects of their message. But each was responsible for speaking it. After all, if Ezekiel, Paul, and Jesus met with opposition, why shouldn't those who claim having met Jesus as a credential?

We pause now to pray silently for the courage to speak the truth . . . and not to put it past the members of our own household to be the voice of God.

2.

Truth and Consequences: Beyond the Comfort Zone

Jeremiah 1:4-5; 17-19
Luke 4:21-30

We church-goers sometimes resemble grocery-shoppers. We tend to pick and choose which values and dreams of Jesus we'll buy . . . and would like to leave the rest on the shelf or between the covers of Scripture! But somehow, the lectionary does not let us do selective shopping in God's Word! Some weekends we're faced with a cart full of items we'd rather not select: the challenges and risks that believers—people growing in faith and commitment—need to look at and act upon. Today is one of those times.

Our Gospel and first reading both illustrate how speaking out, telling the truth, can be costly. Maybe the price is steep because truth is so rare! But whatever the reason, truth can be a dangerous thing and opposition often follows.

Let's look at truth and consequences for Jesus. He ruffles enough feathers early in His ministry to provoke people to want to lynch Him. But it's far too early for Jerusalem. Here He is, in His hometown synagogue, where the expectations of the native son's sermon are nostalgia and good feelings. But instead, His former neighbors get a warning: The God of Israel has *extended* healing and salvation to Gentiles, foreigners, men and women from Sidon and Syria, and passed *you* up because you rejected the prophets and took being chosen for granted! So God had to go *beyond the parochial*—we'd say outside the parish boundaries or county line—to extend the Good News to the vulnerable who knew they needed it! "Charity begins at home" didn't work, so God offered it elsewhere with better results!

What a mouthful of truth! And how did His neighbors respond?

- It's not fair! We're number one!
- Who does He think He is? We grew up with Him!
- Let's get rid of Him!

Suddenly the native son with the silver tongue threatens their comfort zone, violating territorial boundaries. Their small-mindedness turns to rage!

We tend to push our prophets out of sight when they make us feel uncomfortable. How does this look today, and how does rage from the comfort zone happen? Just last week I read a story that shows this sin against prophets who speak the truth. It had to do with Brazilian bishops who turned from prestige and took a stance for the poor, working with them and advocating for change. With that and the parallel growth of base communities, faith was wedded to justice and the Church flourished. But as the bishops shared their stories of ministry among God's little ones, a tragic consequence resulted. A protest demonstration was held at which bishops joined workers who sought a raise from 25¢ to 28¢ an hour. Police turned a bishop's Volkswagen upside down, beat him nearly to death, stripped him, poured a bucket of red paint over his body, and dumped him on a street corner. The people nursed him back to health and now he tells of what it is like to be anointed like Jesus to bring Good News to the poor! He was a threat to the comfort zone!

But what about us? When is speaking the truth costly? We've heard about folks who blow the whistle on corporations' hazardous waste and end up dead. Our stories are as important but maybe less dramatic:

You're at a party and somebody from your school or workplace—a foreigner by point of view or birth-place—is the topic of ridicule. You know better but at first hesitate to contradict it. Then courage enters your heart and you speak your truth. What happens? Maybe nothing. Maybe you're left to fend for yourself the next time a party is held. Maybe you lose a friend or two or don't get a raise. Whatever the consequences, you are aware that the cost of speaking the truth is high.

But you believe that love prevails over parochialism, and that's what motivated your speech. So Jeremiah, Jesus, and you accepted outcasts and became outcasts. But eventually the truth sets us all free. In fact, when Jesus escapes through the crowd at the cliff-hanger of this Gospel scenario, He is predicting the Easter mystery, when He broke through death itself!

Today we place in our shopping carts a slice of Jesus' values that we'd rather leave on the shelf. But people willing to *consume* this piece of the message will find themselves empowered by God for both the truth and the consequences. It's part of growing up in the faith to narrow the gulf between the comfort zone and foreign territory. And God visited foreign territory long before *we* ever thought of going there!

IN

we tame our demons

THE

there is no hiding place

DESERT

one meets god's power to save

COME

BREAK THE ICE

TO

quench **THIRST**

THE

tap into your inner wellspring

WELL

UNLOOSE THE FOUNTAIN

LENTEN REFLECTIONS

1.

Ashes under Our Nails: Lent as Sorting Time

Joel 2:12-18

Ten Augusts ago, my parents experienced a house fire in our family home. Since I lived only eight blocks away at the time, I rushed over there as soon as I received the call. After the neighbors had all gone home and the equipment was removed, the Battalion Chief brought us three metal garbage containers full of the charred items his team had shoveled out of the front closet where the fire originated. He said sometimes people find important things they want to keep.

So together on the back lawn we fingered through three large barrels of ashes before dusk settled. We laughed and we cried. We remembered—and we died. All of a sudden we'd spot a swatch of material: the lining of Dad's hat or the hem of Mom's robe! And halfway down we found an old prayer-book with a note I had written my mother in 1958 as a fifth grader: "Pray for me, Mom. Love, Janie." We found an alligator purse in which there were precious photos. That night we literally sorted through our past. We let go of some good but unnecessary things and found some we could keep. And we all changed inside.

Then the neighbors came back (the kitchen, luckily, wasn't boarded up) and Dad served beer and pretzels. Later, despite all the invitations to stay with others overnight, my folks decided to remain in the back of the very damaged house—and would stay there for the many months it took to repair the rest.

The part that needed refurbishing was boarded up, darkened from the outside to the inside. There were no distractions; we could see what was on the inside. And there followed tedious days of putting our house in order, one step at a time.

I returned to the parish where I lived around midnight, and as I typed a list of the destroyed items for the insurance company, I thought, "What a change this night will mean for us!" I had *ashes* under my nails for three weeks as one reminder. Life went on, but its quality and depth were very different. We didn't take God or home or each other for granted after that and recognized the beauty in other people's goodness again.

Today our church offers us a season, initiated as we bless ourselves with *ashes*, a time to sort through who we are in the sight of God and who we strive to be in Jesus' name. We are given helps, standard means, that aid us in deciding what must go and what is worth keeping: prayer, fasting, and alms-giving. And amid the ashes, we'll discover selfishness—but also the will to nurture wholesome relationships. We'll find shaky faith—but the desire to turn to God more eagerly for direction in life. We'll see hesitation to reach out if we know it will be demanding but the good will to keep trying anyhow. In short, we'll discover sin and virtue, and we'll laugh and cry and die a little. But we will surely change inside. And we'll not leave that place, that darkened room with few distractions. We'll have the *"ashes under our nails"* from today to remind us we're putting our house in order.

And after we've been faithful during the Lenten season of sorting and letting go and keeping, we'll call in the neighbors and celebrate at Easter that we've died and risen in the manner of Jesus. And life will go on, but its quality and depth will be permanently changed. Keep those ashes under your nails!

2.

Spotting the Wolves: What Little Red Riding Hood and Jesus Have in Common

Matthew 4:1-11

Recently I was reading about a former pre-school teacher who recalled many things her students' parents did not want their darlings exposed to during the school day: raisins, chocolate, Kool Aid . . . and the character of the *big bad wolf* when she read *Little Red Riding Hood!* But this wise woman felt it was important to teach children to spot the wolves dressed like grandmas, to distinguish the "Come closer, dear" of relatives from the deceptive voices that could lure them toward danger.

In today's Gospel scenario, Jesus spots the wolf dressed like Grandma. He is newly baptized and struggling to sort out the voices of good and evil. And He walks away with a deeper sense of who He is and what He's about.

But why the desert as the arena for this confrontation? Because in the desert there is no hiding place, none of the comforts of home. There, one faces one's naked need, one's desperate hunger for security. There one cannot pretend. Maya Angelou has The Rock cry out in her inaugural poem: "Seek no haven in my shadow . . . I will give you no hiding place!"

All the great religious prophets went to such places before they taught their followers what truth they found: Buddha to the wilderness of India, Mohammed to the desert of Saudi Arabia, and Jesus to the sands of Palestine. The desert, after all, is where the heart is vulnerable, where broken people stare at the Infinite and allow God to penetrate the deep crevices of their human spirit. In the desert, we see illusions for what they are. In the desert, we begin to tame the demons that get between us and loving relationships. In the desert, our need meets God's power to save.

It is in the desert, then, that Jesus faced what all baptized sons and daughters of God face: those subtle and deceptive voices outside ourselves that try to define us. Those voices cheapen baptismal grace and abuse God's Word by suggesting painless shortcuts and convenient means to make *ourselves* the center of our lives, rather than the God Whose daughter or son we are.

Now Jesus' approach to evil is not evasion but a steady look at it as empty idolatry. When the Tempter puts a condition on His identity ("If you are God's Chosen one. . ."), all that Jesus says is proof that He is, and a faithful one at that. And when the Tempter uses God's own Word, Jesus' source of strength, to render Him weak, Jesus attacks fundamentalist manipulation of the Word with a grounded understanding of God's help at every turn. Evil is not the last word. And the wolf, once spotted, did not, in the end, get the better of Grandma!

It's Lent. We need to create a desert, that solitary place where we can name and confront the wolves dressed like Grandma, those idols subtly trying to define us from the outside, the lures to laurels that make *us* the center of our lives. Where are the wolves dressed like Grandma?

- Many subtle television ads which urge us to love *things* and use *people* and never make altruism look attractive.
- The mentality of "love—if it works out" or love with "what-do-I-get-out-of-it" strings attached.
- The powerful "I-need-to-be-right syndrome" which keeps one up, one down in relationships.
- The "more-is-better" mentality which clouds our vision.

. . . and last but never least of deceptive voices,

- our own self-hate couched in nasty put-downs directed at ourselves when we forget our dignity as God's own.

All of these wolves dressed like Grandma keep us from trusting God, ourselves, and each other.

The temptations of Jesus remind us of our identity as children of God and our source of truth as God's Word. This Lent, let's steep ourselves in that dignified identity and not let any wolf have the last word! Let's allow whatever tests us make us strong and real and holy. Let's *banish the wolf* and *embrace Grandma*!

3.

Calluses, Empty Eyes and a Thirst for Jesus: Meet You at the Well!

John 4:5-42

I used to work in a small rural Mississippi town. One of the things I miss most is the post office! It's located in the center of activity, near the largest grocery and the Church of Christ. When a person stops in for mail, she encounters every sort of uniform: baker's, clergy's, laundry clerk's, farmer's, and factory worker's. Patrons there represent every race in town, every age and neighborhood. There are college kids from the nearby campus. And ecumenism is at its best on the parking lot, where the Methodist organist chats with the Lutheran minister's wife, and the Catholic parish council president stops to greet the newly-ordained Episcopal woman pastor!

There, at the post office, a common need brings people together, and in the process of doing business, these folks reassure each other and make vital connections. I used to watch elderly citizens walk away with no mail but smiling broadly from the social exchanges. Some days I found myself back home, mailbox key in hand, having forgotten to pick up the mail, which was why I had gone! A lot happens at the post office.

In Palestine, the village well held similar importance. Moses and Jacob met their wives at a well. And in Jesus' day, women carried the household's large stone water jars there three times a day, hoisting them atop shoulders and head and bringing the rope and buckets with which to draw the precious water. Visitors and strangers *had* to ask for water, as residents alone had the equipment to carry it.

Remember as we speak of the "woman at the well" that the culture of Jesus' day encouraged Jews to express hostility to Samaritans, a habit that had persisted for 700 years. If one entered their territory, they were to avoid contact, maybe as we avoid eye contact in elevators without even thinking about it!

So what happened at this well that made its way into the pages of Scripture and has mystified believers for centuries? Sin met grace, and the water jar was forgotten. Jesus broke gender and culture and racial taboos and became for one willing Samaritan, and eventually her whole village, the Savior of the world! One noon, a woman drawing water became a credible apostle and shifted the focus of her worship!

The Samaritan woman had skeletons in her closet, as do all of us who have lived as long; the initial weapon she used on Jesus, the thirsty Jewish stranger, was sarcasm. After all, she'd had enough men dipping into her resources all these years! But Jesus was undaunted in His pursuit. He seemed to see her calluses, noticed her empty eyes, and somehow knew the issue for her was not the physical thirst, buckets, temples, and ancestry, about which they spoke.

Jesus leads her to name the demons but keeps His eyes of mercy on her all the while. He gives her a reason to live that would tap into the wellspring inside, instead of leaving her unsatisfied and lonely. He simply sees her and loves her.

Sometimes I think we have exaggerated the personal sin of this woman and ourselves too much, to the exclusion of the social evil that's harder to handle and root out. Here, hatred and exclusion, isolation and discrimination permeate her culture with the same magnitude that ethnic cleansing and covert forms of prejudice saturate ours today. In a moment's question, Jesus broke through the barriers of sex and race that had a crusty history and deep animosity attached to them.

Notice how the disciples stood apart, probably half admiring and half afraid. But the woman's life is flowing, and her enthusiasm bubbles up so genuinely, she becomes believable to her own people. No longer is the well's water an afternoon's agenda. Now she has met One who knows and loves her, teaches people that worship begins inside, and sees no need to uphold traditions that divide her people and His.

Jesus knows that *sin* is keeps people thirsty—for acceptance, for inclusion, for reassurance, for forgiveness and a new start. He also knows that conversion involves facing a loving Lord (calluses, empty eyes, demons and all) to be known and challenged. And for her, accepting forgiveness included running free to spread the News that power is available in His name.

This is our story as well. As infants, most of us were baptized at the common well of the church's sacramental pool. We return to the source of life often, and renew each Lent the promise to dip into that life we share with God, to encounter the Savior Who sees our calluses and empty eyes, and Who knows the demons that strive to claim us. And in that exchange, we are refreshed and empowered to witness that we don't any longer find life in prejudice and can get along without the bucket!

Meet you at the well!

4.

DRAWN TO WATER: ACCESS TO AN ENORMOUS MERCY

John 4:5-42

I have always been drawn to water and have lived in four states, always near significant bodies of water: Lake Michigan, the Menomonee River, the Mississippi River, and the Saginaw River. Access to these meant refreshment: fishing, hiking, and picnics. And when mourning or dealing with deep disappointment, I would find in these waters a place of comfort and healing.

The waters with the least appeal for me have been stagnant and frozen bodies of water. On these, no movement is visible, access is difficult, and there is little I find inviting.

Today in the Gospel we heard of a woman drawn to water out of need. But she finds deeper refreshment than she dared expect! It was high noon when this marginated Samaritan outcast, an unclean woman, came to draw. (No crowd because her more *reputable* peers came earlier in the morning, before the sun was high.)

Access was easy with bucket and rope. But then along comes a Jew, a man, thirsty as she, trodding on enemy territory and suggesting they share a common cup! (If she is unclean, he will be, too!) This gesture breaks the ice of deep hatred based on religious differences between their two cultures, an icy, stagnant stance she would at first try to sustain with sarcasm, defensiveness, and theological debate.

He asks simple questions and leads her to deeper ones. She speaks of buckets and wells; He shows a mercy so generous she forgets why she'd come. He could have thrown her past and the infidelity of her culture in her face with a violence that would shatter her minute self-respect in an instant. Instead, it is named and redeemed and the cold front melts. All this by the mercy of a Savior-God Who did not invent barriers!

And how? How *is* conversion and salvation experienced? By conversation that engages her with the love of God. By an exchange that invites her to locate a fountain within that needs neither bucket nor well, which when unloosed will evangelize the town before daybreak! Now that's Good News!

Lent is our time to be renewed in the enormous sea of God's mercy, a sea with access. But we're asked to do what she did: look carefully at our lives and those of our church and society to see where we've blocked access to ourselves and others. To see where we've kept others in a cold, thirsty, or stagnant situation. Where have we kept grace from flowing? Where have we posted *"Private! Keep Out"* signs on the way our neighbor walks? Where have we set boundaries where God's mercy wants access to the human heart?

Boundaries. Categories. Stereotypes: deep, cold chasms forged by people who can't imagine a sea of mercy because they live in a culture iced-over by years of hostility: Palestinian/Jew in Israel, Protestant/Catholic in Northern Ireland, Majority/Minority in South Africa . . . people whose lives are erased as if they didn't matter.

Keep Out! No Access: Church structures that keep some of the baptized from ministry because of encrusted traditions or gender preferences.

Private Club! Whites Only! Membership Card Required! And some die of thirst while a sea of mercy is available.

Keep Out! The sign we raise when we throw people's past infidelities in their face, giving them ashes instead of a fountain. *Thirsts* of many kinds.

And how did Jesus break through with the ocean of mercy He is? *Conversation! Imagine that!* A presence that did not go away . . . a respect as uncommon as the well was common!

Can we pay the price of mercy-filled conversation this Lent? Can we invest the trust? I believe we are here to say, "Yes!" I believe we are here to pray that we and the whole world can get beyond the stagnation and ice of sin, and to admit these evils in order to be freed of their power.

Welcome to the ocean of God's mercy!

5.

The Blind Man and the Green Bowl: The Miracle of More-than-Meets-the-Eye

John 9:1-41

I have an object here. I'd like you to tell me what you see. (Assembly calls out a response.) Yes, it is a green bowl with a crack in it. Not especially beautiful, certainly not modern or practical as a Teflon or stainless steel one would be. It's breakable. There's really nothing amazing about it.

But let's look at the bowl this way: It was the bread-mixing bowl my mother used each Saturday as I grew up. After she died, I moved to Mississippi, where I prepared potluck foods in it, and carried it on my lap to parish gatherings so it wouldn't break. Then, when I moved to Michigan, I packed it with great care because for me it is a sacred object filled with family tradition.

There! Now you see with both *your eyes* and at least *my heart*! You see, there was more to this bowl than you thought! And you believed me when I told you this green bowl has a life all its own!

Lent is a time we choose to see "the more" with the eyes of the heart. Jesus is the catalyst for us believers because His miracles in us cause us to question old ways of seeing. And there's usually lots of confusion before the clarity comes.

Take today's Gospel about the process of moving from blindness to sight: It's about not seeing the light. It's about being afraid to see the light. It's about seeing the light. It's about refusing to see the light. It's also about looking but not seeing, and seeing what was there before but never perceived. It's about God loving so much that Jesus can use blindness as an opening for a breakthrough! It's about the reign of God reversing a long-held belief: that physical defects are punishment for sin! It's about mud becoming salve and water washing a humiliating past away. It's about what happens when Jesus notices, characteristically cares, and acts with the power of God to create us anew!

Last week our homilist said we usually want to change people, and then we'll accept them . . . but that Jesus does it the other way: He accepts people and when they receive that, they change! The blind beggar was touched by Jesus, and that's when all heaven broke loose! But people around him were reluctant to believe in miracles, so confusion and society's sin broke loose, too!

Three prominent groups closed their eyes: Some Pharisees, who represent our *legalism*, claimed this was impossible because the man is a sinner and we don't allow cures on the Sabbath. The man's parents, who represent our *cynicism*, fear, and cowardice, said they wanted to stay out of it. They passed the shekel! And the bystanders, who represent our *skepticism*, figured he musn't have been blind before. After all, there's a scientific explanation for everything!

Blindness in this Gospel is a moral disease. It thrives on a ho-hum attitude about what we get used to. It grows when we don't claim the love God offers, when we filter miracles through our minds so they never touch our hearts! It concludes tragically that the Good News is just *too* good to be true, so we'll just stay in the dark. This Gospel shows how miracles don't prove anything to those who don't *want* to believe! And that can happen to us when we allow legalism, cynicism, and skepticism to blur the miracles!

But the good news is that we can also respond like the blind beggar when we allow our eyes to see what Jesus does. The man both saw the light, and saw that Jesus is Light of the World. He didn't understand how Jesus gave him sight (notice the repeated phrase, "I have no idea!"), but he knew a miracle when he *saw* one! And he knew that only God could be behind something as transforming as that!

I often feel that way when I watch parishioners evolve in their ministries . . . first hesitant even to try, then mildly enthused, then becoming confident, and finally, remarkably hungry for more, like retreats and books! Only *God* could be behind something so transforming, I often think! And we respond to the miracle in the only way the blind man could: with awe and worship and with the conviction we witness!

Our Lenten practices of prayer, fasting, and alms-giving are all designed to help us see straight, unblur our vision, so we can see the miracles. If we don't, we may choose the slavery of staying in the dark! But be aware! Corrected vision means *seeing beyond*, and the insight Jesus offers comes with a cost! Just as sunlight and electricity show us what was already there but unnoticed, so will new vision open us to see the hurts that need healing, the relationships that need reconciling. Awakenings are painfully freeing!

We pray today to leave the ho-hum familiarity of what we're used to seeing and enter the transforming presence of the Light of the World, where green bowls aren't just for mixing, and where miracles happen for anyone with the *heart* to see!

Lazarus: Jesus Restores a Stinking Friend!

John 11:1-45

Lazarus was so dead he stunk!

Martha and Mary's grief was so normal they grumbled . . . and used the "W" word: *why* didn't you come through for us, Jesus, when we needed you most?

Jesus loved so deeply He wept . . . for His friend, but also because the power of death had become too strong in the world! And out of this seemingly irreversible chaos came *life* because Jesus gathered His resources and those of the community to *reverse* chaos!

What were those resources Jesus tapped? The power of God within Him, a creative power that brings life out of chaos. And the community's shared compassion, as they helped move the stone and unwrap the shrouded Lazarus. *Together* they opened the grave. How horrifying because it involved facing the demon death and defying it!

Lazarus means "helpless one"—not just this one, but the many we meet through contact with television, newspapers, our parish family, and home. Now, as the assembled Body of Christ, we do what Jesus did. We will visit five tombs and call the bound out to life and liberation!

First, we visit the tomb of a mother in Bosnia. She had been raped by seven soldiers, and her four-year-old was as well. *Her dignity had died.* We shout to her with all that is in us:

"Lazarus, come out!"

Next, we visit a fifteen-year-old boy from our own city who has been ripping the passenger seats in the local buses because he is angry at his folks, the school system, and his friends. Now the elderly are afraid to ride the buses. And really, no one wins in a situation like this. *His youth and innocence are dead.* We invite him back to joy as convincingly as we can:

"Lazarus, come out!"

We also visit a widow who hates the loneliness and has finally just stopped eating. *Her reason for living is dead.* We encourage her with our plea:

"Lazarus, come out!"

Fourth, we view many married couples so used to each other they seldom show affection, affirm one another, or thank. *Their union is dying.* And because we believe love is meant to last forever, we cry out:

"Lazarus, come out!"

Our last tomb is the largest and oldest . . . the institutional church. She has been both graced and sinful, and a hungry media won't let us forget that. She is our mother; hers is our shame as well. This body has wronged and been wronged. *Her credibility is dying.* We are compelled to scream for our own sakes:

"Lazarus, come out!"

In conclusion, I would like to tell you about a man I met at a Michigan Pax Christi meeting. He was debilitated but dragged his body to the microphone. He told the story of being labeled, and as he did, another man composed his life at the piano into a tragically beautiful song. And when the piece was sung, the speaker lifted his head. His face glowed as he said, "I came here today an aching old man, but I go away alive again!"

Jesus still restores life to His friends!

7.

Fickle Hosanna Crowds: Milwaukee and Jerusalem

Mark 11:1-10

There was only one time my mother let us kids skip school. It was in 1958 when the then Milwaukee Braves won the pennant and would be in the World Series! Milwaukee hosted a huge parade downtown to welcome the victors home . . . and we went.

It was a long wait. I craned my neck to see my favorite players, knowing they made the city proud and did something rare and wonderful. I felt the power of the *crowd*: the noise, the numbers, and how everyone moved together as one person. We screamed in what seemed like one voice, a celebration in unison!

Today our Gospel describes another parade and *crowd*: the people assembled in the holy city of Jerusalem during Passover Festival. It was a mix of pilgrims and natives who spoke with a variety of accents different from the Galilean one Jesus was used to hearing.

Mark tells us Jesus Himself engineered this parade, preparing the humble transport and knowing the route. But this event was more than Jesus' physical arrival in a city far south of where He had done most of His teaching and healing. It was the beginning of the final scenario, the beginning of the end, a celebration of the completion of three years of ministry. That mission was now accomplished. This marked the final embrace of all He was and could do for us, and we see Him ride it out with *passion*.

To live passionately is to exert influence on life, affect people and events, and be affected by them in significant ways. To be passive is to have things done to you. And we see why this reading is proclaimed on Passion Sunday. For this parade would leave no doubt for His opposition as to where to find Him for the arrest.

That was the scenario. And how did the crowd respond? They were in the mood for festival, loudly filling the streets and talking about the marvel Jesus had recently worked by curing the blind man. They see their Deliverer fresh from that miracle and are full of faith, so with great enthusiasm proclaim Him hero and triumphant Messiah of God. This, my sisters and brothers, was the "secret" Mark's Jesus had refused to let them speak . . . until the time came. And this was the time.

So they became a "Hosanna" crowd. Hosanna means "Save now!" and had been used for pleading in times of distress but now for sheer, unabashed praise. Imagine the crowd's thoughts whirling, envisioning Him as the anointed sovereign of the realm of the future. Their hearts were throbbing with loyalty, welcome, and homage! In the rows of people were some who yelled, "You healed my baby! Remember me?" or "He made me whole again!" And the prostitute said, "This man made me feel forgiven by even the God of Israel!" Parents shouted, "Everything you taught us on the hill we repeat to our children!" They cheered, and the rally was deafening with praise!

And we? We are there, too, amidst the believers, yelling "Hosanna!" as we recall the health He restored, the peace revived, the relationships mended, the strength He's lent our lives. *Hosanna!* a hundred times over!

And how does this popular Savior react? He neither eggs the crowd on nor ignores it, but keeps on moving, knowing that this is not the end of the story. He is both Host and Guest, exhilarated but reserving somber thought to Himself about where all this "going public" will lead. For Jesus knew what we now know: *Crowds* are fickle. Those who cheer today may jeer tomorrow. Once the Braves short stop missed a line drive or a runner was tagged before reaching home plate, the fans who had gone wild throwing confetti downtown turned to boos and hisses!

And that's how the hosanna crowd became the "Crucify Him!" crowd of today's Passion account. Fear and forgetfulness overwhelm the praise until opposition mounts to a fever pitch. And once the cross replaces the marvels, Jesus is too much for them. Sometimes we're in that crowd, too. We give up as soon as disappointment comes, or praise Jesus for dying but show little concern for where His Body bleeds today!

This is "Hosanna!" day. With the crowd, we acknowledge that in Jesus we experience salvation. Let's commit ourselves to a "passionate" Holy Week and Christian life—one in which we allow ourselves to be stirred to the depths by Jesus' faithfulness, and more eager than ever to believe that all who bear His name must ride through tragedy to experience glory!

8.

A Fractured World: Cross-beams of Redemption (An Ecumenical Good Friday Sermon)

Isaiah 52:13-53
John 12:18-19

Ours is a fractured world. The media tells us how to think and vote. Advertisers convince us that what we want is really what we need. Democracy is fragile. Relationships are tentative. And the human spirit is troubled by a gnawing desire for the Perfect Love.

It is into this forum of greed and need, of buying and selling, into this culture seeking cheap answers to sacred questions, that a Savior, a cross, and a bloody death fit-for-a-criminal, burst into our memories with love and poignancy. Into this arena of scarce human faithfulness and fragile human dreams enters the reminder that a Son stayed attuned to God's plan to the extent of execution.

Isaiah describes a Servant so amazing, so self-effacing, that He was shunned as an oddity. Despite His peaceable nature, violence of the worst kind was done to Him. And it was in this manner that He became Savior of this very fragile, very fractured world. So we gather tonight to remember, to celebrate, to honor the world's greatest Lover.

Isaiah's reminder is haunting: "He has borne our infirmities and carried our diseases." An experience I had last spring put flesh on that description from the Fourth Suffering Servant Song. One of our very active, very loving parishioners underwent a serious heart surgery and after returning home had a relapse. I was called to the hospital after he was re-admitted. First, I did all of the usual things: listening, holding a hand, and prayer. But I still felt helpless and said, "I wish there were more I could do for you." And Larry, usually full of fun, responded quickly and with utter seriousness in a way that startled me: "You could exchange places with me!"

Suddenly, I was stunned by the thought that my commitment could become a risky journey to the brink of death. I was humbled by the knowledge that *that* cost was just *too high.* After all, bearing his infirmities would slow me down, adjust my relationships, down-size my options, and certainly disturb my well-learned time management! I simply was not ready to pour myself out that way for Larry. There were limits. And every muscle in my stomach tightened as I stood next to his bed, knowing how much we both needed a Savior!

Indeed, this is a fractured world of fragile loves! I am sure we have known this feeling when we have chosen to take the position of Peter in John's Passion account: standing outside, staying safe, keeping our distance. We know instinctively the cost of *passion*: having things done to us . . . letting bad things happen to the best of good people . . . and Larry was one!

At times like that, we want no one to read our fear. The moment of truth would be glaring in its starkness. The fact is, no degree of commitment among even the holiest of Jesus' followers could compare to the unconditional love of God in the unwavering faithfulness of Jesus. His humble restraint and decisive resolution to love us to the finish are unmatched much as we can spend our lives trying to imitate them! In Jesus, the very authority of God rose up with the force of a heavenly power to assure Him of the integrity of truth and the ultimate value of death for those who believe.

John's account attests to the fact that one of Jesus' parting gestures before dying was giving mother and friends to each other, creating a community of disciples as He gave over the Spirit that would keep it alive. How fitting that belonging to each other became a fruit of the victory of the cross! The otherwise fractured world becomes a community whose memory still holds Jesus dear, a universal community that acknowledges that Jesus is Savior of the whole world!

Now our churches would never require us to gaze lovingly on an electric chair or replica of a guillotine. Instead, they invite us to embrace the cross: healing instrument of Divine mercy, shrine of the lavish love of a Wounded Healer! What for many has been a hideous symbol of Roman torture has become for us a powerful reminder of God's overwhelming desire to save!

When our dying means we lose control and wrenches our spirit, we remember the cross-beams:

- When your children finally ride the two-wheeler you've taught them to ride, and suddenly their independence fills you with emptiness, you recall the freedom the cross won.
- When your spouse is diagnosed with cancer just as the two of you begin to enjoy a well-deserved retirement, you feel the regret of Peter, the despair of Judas.
- When your daughter chooses a spouse you find difficulty welcoming into the family, you remember "Here is your son!" And, the cost of following is high.

It is then, brothers and sisters, that we are united with the one Whose love knows no bounds, the only One Who can teach us everything . . . even how to *die*!

9.

Redemptive Diminishment: The Gift of Jesus' Death (An Ecumenical Good Friday Sermon)

John 18-19

There is nothing more real than death. I was with my father last October as he experienced his, and it was so real that all six of us in the room were literally struck dumb with awe for the 45 minutes that followed. All of a sudden six otherwise vocal people were reduced to the profoundest silence, a silence filled with sadness, relief, mystery, loss, love, exhaustion, and, yes, faith. There is nothing more real than death.

And there is nothing more beautiful than death for others, a sacrificial act of love, the ultimate giving by giving up. In Catholic circles, one way we understand that gesture of Jesus is by re-telling the story of Maximillian Kolbe, a German-Jew turned priest. Kolbe found himself in a concentration camp as the cell mate of a young husband and father whose number was called—for death by starvation. The man had shared with Kolbe his dread of death, so when the guards came, Kolbe convinced them to take him instead. Imagine the guards' shock, the disbelief of the man, and the full, rich love of Kolbe! And imagine yourself, ransomed today by the innocent Lamb of God.

Jesus and Kolbe did remarkable things: choosing to suffer not out of weakness but from the fullness of love. And that love gave life! The love of Jesus in suffering was an act of mercy blotting out selfishness, an act of healing to bring comfort, a choice with redemptive value.

But Jesus' death was also "passive," that is, it involved "being done to," being "delivered into the hands of" and losing control. Execution on trumped-up charges is among the most securely established facts of His life. As innocent victim, he experienced the distress and isolation any person would because of His full capacity for humanity within an equally divine nature. He was guilty only of faithfulness. What a splendid charge! What a tragic reason to die!

Now we are among those saved both by Jesus' choice and His submission to passivity within that process. I issue two challenges to us who meditate on the mystery of the cross today. The first is emulation of His suffering, willingness to die a little every day. That always looks like losing control, and is. Your employer publicly criticizes your best efforts. But does your value hinge upon performance? Your elderly parent is embarrassed in the nursing home dining room because he drools or has frequent coughing spells that hinder his social life. And you can't seem to come up with the right word of encouragement. Or you try to convince your spouse or child of your unconditional love, but again and again your words fall short of your good intention.

These are all examples of the "redemptive diminishment" our limits impose, the experience of our limits being able to heal us, if only our faith will remind us of the dear cost of discipleship.

The second challenge I would lay out is active solidarity with our suffering brothers and sisters as a sign of atonement, or more properly, at-one-ment. We are, unfortunately, prone to deciding just who is deserving of our attention, service, and affection. We are, all of us, ransomed, yet pain still surrounds us like a virus. And to look on the cross and notice the still broken Body of Christ in our world must be parallel acts of reverence. Who is despised today, given over to shameful treatment? Is it crack and coke babies? Hungry children? Single parents exhausted from working and raising the children alone? Is it people sleeping in the streets, refugees seeking a home? Is it that annoying relative craving a gentle word? A youth who presents a hard front but who represents the most suicidal group in America? Is it the caretakers of the sick who need a break? These are among the many who cry out, "My God, my God, why have You abandoned me?" Our suffering must arise out of active solidarity with them, or Jesus' death remains an empty gesture.

In the words of Anthony Padovano, "People come of age when they suffer because they have seen the right things. They suffer not because they are physically assaulted or violent others seek to injure them. They suffer because of their beliefs. They suffer because of their promises. They suffer not because of what they have done, but because of who Jesus is." (*Dawn without Darkness*, p. 65)

If we learn to accept the limits of redemptive diminishment and live in active solidarity with the still suffering Body of Christ, we signal to all the world that Jesus' cross truly set us free. If not, we are like the crowd of bystanders at Jesus' crucifixion who only followed at a distance. Amen.

BREAKTHROUGH

JESUS BROKE THROUGH

WALKED RIGHT IN

share your fears

GROW IN INTIMACY

WHEN DO OUR HEARTS BURN?

RUN

tell everyone **WHO** you've met

(there's no limit to meeting places)

PEACE BE WITH YOU

JESUS

i will never **IS** leave you orphans

RISEN

JESUS

best of good shepherds

YOU BELONG TO ME

THE VINE

PRUNING

ASSURES

FRUITFULNESS

CELEBRATING THE RISEN JESUS

1.

Fears Shared: Becoming an Easter People

Acts 2:42-47
John 20:19-31

Fear can really bring people together! Think of when the electricity goes out and children run instinctively to their parents. When I worked in the Mississippi Delta, the lights failed frequently, and we all gathered with our candles! Or when miners are trapped or loved ones are kidnapped and as yet unfound, what is the first thing most of us do? We seek the company of the comforting; we need someone to tell.

Fears shared can bring a closeness. I remember once I was in my office and a woman on our staff whom I had always admired for her courage walked in with her coffee cup. Before long, she admitted in a tiny voice her intense fear of the dark! We grow in intimacy when we share our fears or hear others'!

Today's first and third readings give us a human portrait of the early Christian community, those closest to Jesus before He rose. Their strong fear is the focus, since they only understand they *don't* understand the resurrection! They only know for sure that they're *not* sure what Jesus' rising will mean for them. These are the famous and very frightened saints—Thomas, Peter, John, and Nathaniel—who simply shake with fear! Let's look at their fears—and ours. Let's examine what the Lord did with theirs, and will do with ours as well.

In our passage from Acts, the disciples are filled with awe, speechless, because through them, the risen Lord has worked wonders among the people. God has shared the power of miracles with them as they work in His name. Their response? Scared to death! Stupefied!

So what did they do? They banded together, prayed, ate and worked together, continued Jesus' values, and gave generously to the poor. Their fear resulted in community and ministry! Not so bad—for fear!

And what of us? Our fear can also arise out of not understanding the circumstances of our lives—a turn of fortune, a failure, a loss. Fear is created when we are uncertain and suddenly insecure. And we do what the disciples did: come together to *look at it* with eyes of faith and *get beyond it* by serving yet other fearful people! When folks tell me they can worship God as well at home, I wonder, "What about all the energy, inspiration, and help that comes from bringing our fear and faith together?" The Scriptures say this is our tradition, starting with Jesus and His own and then those who witnessed Jesus risen. And they were scared!

A second type of fear is based on knowing the risks involved in following Jesus. The disciples actually locked themselves in, afraid to stick their necks out too far for the Jewish leaders to see. Besides fear of authority, they feared for life and reputation. And what resulted from this fear? Jesus Himself broke through, walking right into the midst of it with the original greeting of peace! And not only that! He also unleashed in them the power to free others from all that kept them bound.

We have lots of locked doors. We keep new ideas out because they would demand too much change of us. We restrict people from getting inside because they challenge us—or keep loving us, even when we feel unworthy! We stay on the beaten path because it's just easier. And what does Jesus do? He walks right in and says, "I'm with you." He allows a crisis, an opportunity, a friendship, a grace, to interrupt the status quo and empower us to risk again, to start over, to believe! Thank goodness, we can't keep Him out!

Lastly, there's Thomas' fear. It is the skepticism of the genuine believer, the doubt of the sincere seeker. He wants to believe, but if he finds out he put his faith in a fraud, he'll be more disappointed than ever! His is the popular "But if" stance! That is, until that famous face-to-face, hand-to-wound encounter which produced the greatest act of faith in the New Testament! He sees and believes.

We, too, calculate the losses. What if we live good lives and find out Jesus isn't what He's cracked up to be? Or what if I had hoped following would be easier, and then He offers me the wounded Body of Christ to touch in sickness or hard times? Will our disappointments be stronger than our faith? Or can we, like Thomas, stay in the company of Jesus' followers long enough to really know Him as Lord and God, as Peace itself?

The lesson from today's three types of fear is that doubt which seeks the truth can be greater than blind faith. Faith and fear are not opposites. Fear admitted and transformed as we meet the risen Lord is part and parcel of both holiness and credible discipleship! Alleluia!

2.

Risen Lord, Is There Anywhere You're Not?

Luke 24:13-35

What do these events of my past week have in common?
- riding a tractor cutting fresh, aromatic grass with the wind blowing through my hair;
- holding a four-month-old baby just up from her nap;
- eating fresh turnip greens the same day I picked them;
- singing "Alleluia";
- fishing in a small pond as the wind made ripples on the water;
- hearing you say "Amen!" when I served you the Eucharist;
- kissing the forehead of a very handicapped person and creating a smile.

What connects these events for me is that each was an experience of ordinariness which brought Jesus close, which made Him seem present. Each of these made "my heart burn within me" and was sacred.

Now here are two others: I received a letter that contained disappointment. A good and poor woman became sick and will have to miss work, and a salary, for a month.

Are these, too, signs of Christ present? Yes, but it takes faith to believe that. How can He be present in suffering? It seems these events bring "Where are You, Lord?" rather than "I believe in You, Lord" to most lips!

Our Gospel today begins with a situation more like the second batch of experiences I described. The disciples are broken-hearted and losing hope. Their dreams of Jesus were shattered at the cross. They gripe as they walk and the Stranger catches up with them. They ironically tell Him He must be the most ignorant person around and tell all they know of Him. They find Him a magnetic personality and finally invite Him home. That's where He takes the lead, and in sharing their bread, the Stranger is recognized as the Lord they missed so much!

Then it all makes sense: He had to suffer, but that did not mean He wasn't the Lord. He had to die, but that didn't exclude the possibility of appearing to them transformed but alive! And just when all this became ecstatically clear, He vanished. But from then on, *everything* could remind them of Him, because He was with them more than ever. In fact, He would never leave them again!

Risen, He would not be limited to one physical location. Risen, He would convert their eyes of sight into the vision of faith. And they walk the seven long miles back to Jerusalem—no, they *run*!—to tell everyone Who they met! And no longer is their question to Jesus, "Where are You?" but rather, "Is there anywhere You're *not*?" Their hearts burn within them!

Our experience is not unlike theirs. We walk with the Lord a long journey, sometimes not sensing His presence, and feel dejected. Somebody or something happens and we are shaken to faith, so much so that we're compelled to share good news with others.

Now maybe the lesson is to welcome the stranger. Or maybe it's that sharing our bread can deepen our faith. Or again, maybe it's that in the ordinary, right where we are, is where the risen Lord abides, and we need to invite Him to stay, or our hearts will *never* burn within us.

Oh! One more thing. What do you see here in my hand? It's a piece of the "Berlin Wall" a friend sent from Germany.

Your sight was limited, but a fellow Christian came along and added meaning to what you perceived. This is what the risen Lord did on the road, at the table, and for us when we were on the tractor, holding a baby, and saying "Amen" and "Alleluia." There's just no limit to meeting places when we're in touch with Jesus risen!

3

Will the Real Good Shepherd Please Stand?

John 10:1-10

I've been reading lately about mid-life. Experts say that the first half of our lives, we develop expectations; the second half we alter them! A good example of this for me has been the concept of the Good Shepherd. In grade school, I was given a sentimental, nostalgic picture: white sheep with a tailored shepherd who had shimmering hair and an immaculate robe! Then in the '70s I heard theologian Alfred McBride say that really, shepherds are rump-kickers who deal harshly with some pretty dumb animals! Finally, last year in Israel, I *saw* shepherds. Believe it or not, they were Arab teens wearing jeans and riding donkeys—with transistor radios couched between their shoulders and ears! They herded the flocks from atop the animal, while the adult shepherds hunched down close alongside the sheep, so that I never could get a good photo.

As you can see from these three descriptions, my notion of shepherd has take many turns and been "de-mythologized" over the years of learning and experience. But there's one more piece I just found recently. In preparing this homily, I read that first century shepherds in Palestine were considered unclean because they often violated property rights. They were dishonored and looked down upon. Add to this the recent title "Lamb" given to David Koresh, who led his people to death in Waco, and it's a grim picture!

Jesus could only *restore* the image of shepherd if He referred to Himself as a "Good" one! He was no stranger, but more like shepherds in Palestine now: There is one sheepfold for the region, and all the shepherds bring their flocks to a stone, unroofed corral at night, a place where wild animals and thieves cannot harm them. In the morning, they come back to claim their own sheep. By the distinctive tone of their voices, they are known by the sheep. They call out each one's name: "Longear!" "Whitenose!" etc. Theirs is an intimate rapport!

And that's where we come in. We are baptized Christians, called by name, pastured here in the assembly, nurtured by Word and Eucharist. This is a rich grazing ground, a place of freedom and reassurance where we know we are claimed by Him. But sheep who have grazed are called to pay the price: a life committed to listening to His voice and defending the most defenseless. And in that way, sheep become *shepherds* in the one fold gathered to honor Jesus, best of good shepherds!

4

Branches on the Vine, But More than Just Hanging On

John 15:1-8

Jesus is the Vine, we the branches. Three scenarios:

Imagine yourself a pre-school age child taken to the grocery store by your parent. While there, you are aware of Mother or Dad's lead but wander and look while the parent chooses food that's good for you: cereal, milk, vegetables, etc. Sometimes you stay behind, wondering if an item you choose will be paid for before you both leave for home! At times, your parent rounds a corner and ends up ahead, in a different aisle, but the whole time you are aware of each other and do return home together.

This is one way to understand our life as branches on the vine: following, being guided, having the freedom to choose, and going home with the one who brought us.

A second scenario. Imagine yourself a teenage boy after an evening game. You share stories with peers until the group splits up at the corner. You have two blocks left to walk. It's dark and you're alone now, frightened and trying to talk yourself out of the fear. Finally, you whistle and pick up your pace. In the midst of that, you know in a flash that you aren't alone after all—or ever. Faith tells you that Jesus is one with, is companion to, you. You get home and tell no one that thought, but fleeting as it was, it consoled you. That is another way of being on the vine: never alone, connected even in darkness and fear and when we can't speak of what that is. Comfort happens.

A final scenario. Two elderly women, friends for a lifetime through thick and thin, have occasional coffee but talk on the phone every day. They know the rhythm of each other's lives and how the other would like this food or that television show. There is an easy familiarity, and they are inseparable in spirit, energized just by the thought of how they can count on each other. They live a sort of unspoken communion which even death won't stop. This is more than fellowship or walking with. This is beyond having in mind. This is abiding, residing in. This relationship gives life.

All three images reflect the mystery and wonder of life on the vine . . . and all three *limp*. But they show that discipleship is not exercised in private and that the branches are not only in the company of the vine, but because of the vine, alive together or not at all.

The Gospel text gives us an image that is both tender and comforting. Jesus says, "You belong to me, are part of me, and never *won't* be unless you refuse to stay connected. Draw life from Me and you'll have enough to share in ways that will nourish others, too!"

So often I have seen the effect that nourishment from the vine produces in fruit. At R.C.I.A. gatherings, branches newly-grafted onto the vine affirm the branch-to-branch support. They witness the strength of the connection. Wives and husbands transferred to convalescent centers find strength in their shared faith which is as necessary to their lives as the oxygen they use. Our parish food pantry is an expression of extending the fruit of our common connection to households that are trying to hang on.

The image of pruning is a challenge in this reading. It is both required and costly. I have trouble even cutting off snips from house plants! It always makes them look scrawny and seems at the time counter-productive! But costly as it is, pruning assures fruitfulness. Rupture and failure, loss and even death are often the experiences that bring the greatest growth. But without the benefit of experiencing them in the midst of shared Christian community, they can be bitter challenges to faithfulness indeed! For us who are companions on the journey, pruning often means letting go so collaboration can come about. Consensus and keeping the whole in view can really smart sometimes! Sometimes it means merging projects, or replacing two with one, so more people can be helped. This takes some cutting away of ego and control! If it wouldn't be for our faith in never-ending life from the vine, this pruning process would be just too painful to endure. But the stronger our connection to the life-source, the more potential for fruitful effects of pruning.

We come here because we believe it is not enough to say *I belong to Christ*. We all know that *fruit* is required. Today we are challenged by the Word, both nourished and pruned. And we are fed by the Vine, sharing bread and cup without distinction or preference. Through what we do here, we grow deeply into the very heart of the risen Lord, whose fruits are rich and diversely abundant among us! We are more than hanging on!

5.

Jesus Ascends: It's In Our Hands Now!

Mark 16:15-20

Sometimes the image we have held of this event of Ascension in Jesus' life involves looking at the bottom of His feet as He heads for the clouds! Now it's true that "going up" is important in our culture. We speak of "climbing the ladder of success." Scouts have "flying up" ceremonies when they move to the next level of achievement. We say we need people to "look up to." And we even describe meeting our God in prayer as "going up to the mountain."

But this is really a feast of *fulfillment* for Jesus and one of *mission* for us. On the Ascension, we celebrate Jesus having completed the work God set out for Him. This implies not only that His mission of teaching and healing are completed, but also the entire Paschal Mystery which included conquering sin and death, being raised and returning to show Himself to believers in a new form, and finally returning home to God.

Jesus completed a mission. He was found to be faithful. And God welcomed Him home. Sound familiar? We hear that Peace Corps volunteers do this, medics who attend to victims of disasters across the globe, and missionaries of all sorts. And maybe some of you recall a time when your parents told you they were proud of you and ceremoniously welcomed you home after a major accomplishment. You could relate to this experience of Jesus personally.

But the fact that Jesus finished His work here does not mean that we are orphaned, not does it mean that His work does not go on. No! *We* are entrusted with His mission! We are advised *not* to look in the clouds for Him, but with our feet planted firmly on the ground, to respond to the pain and loneliness we see . . . with *His* love, *His* values, *His* message!

Just what is this Good News we are to take to all people? That they are loved and that the same glory Jesus experienced is possible for them—if only they persevere in hope. And how will they experience hope if we don't show them there's a reason to go on?

Today we are entrusted with Jesus' mission, to carry on where He left off: to be Good News, to produce signs and wonders not by drinking deadly poison but by showing this world that *good* and *God* are more beautiful and powerful, more lasting and fulfilling, than violence and the works of darkness, forces that Jesus' ministry sought to eliminate. We commit ourselves because His mighty work is in *our* hands, and they are up to the task!

6.

Music Man and Jesus' Spirit: Unleashing Our Voice!

John 20:19-23

There's a little character in *Music Man,* a boy who won't speak or socialize, remember? Fear gripped him until he met the Music Man, who taught him to sing and talk and fish and *know joy*!

Such was the situation at Pentecost. People in fear locked themselves away; the followers of Jesus had lost heart. Their Leader had died in capital punishment style, and they had large uncertainties about their future without Him. They were more than afraid to preach in His name. But they gathered to share their fear and memorialize Him by being together . . . like we do weekly. And today we celebrate how that gathering was blessed with an event we know as Pentecost, the dynamic birth of a church with the unleashing of gifts! As we gather, we pray for a continuation of that in our time and place.

Pentecost is an action, a *doing* by Jesus' Spirit, a grand festival of *communication*. What happened? Tongues were loosed in those who had been tongue-tied. Love was freed for sharing. Hope was renewed. Thus, we often see the event depicted with tongues, red flames, and wind!

Our titles for Jesus' Spirit tell us what the Spirit does: Consoler, Advocate, Paraclete, Comforter. One who heals the scars of fear and misunderstanding, brings help and stands with the weak, remains. This Breath of the Living God brings energy, for remember, communicating the *Spirit* of Jesus always involves penetrating what is stuck in what seems an impossible, limited, or dried-up situation with the power that brings life and results in joy! Sometimes this is experienced in an intoxicating way . . . a boisterous out-pouring that brings a flush to the cheek, and joy to a group's spirits. That kind of communication changes a gathering! It allows stretching the limits but not breaking, stepping into risk without falling, creating community but maintaining personality!

What does a *Pentecostal presence* in daily life look like? It is played out when workers get a good idea, a child freely finger-paints, parents make a wise decision, teachers give a helpful response, friends help by being gentle, spouses learn to trust again, and competitors begin to cooperate. It means that a group has the ability to: envision a future with hope, love with inclusion, live faithfully despite uncertainties, see possibilities despite limitations, forgive the way they never thought they could.

What does a *Spirit filled church look like*? It's one in which the love of Christ is not a well-kept secret. It's a place where people freely serve each other, where peace is created, enthusiasm is shared, and growth is always in process! It is where simple gifts are brought to the task of bearing Good News, where prayer is from the heart, and love is from God. Such a church may not always look neat or appear correct, but it is always wise and friendly . . . and alive with hope!

Finally, what does a *renewed face of the earth look like when Pentecost really continues*? The impossible becomes possible! We saw this when the Berlin Wall went down, and every time common citizens decided they would invest time and effort in conserving and preserving our beautiful natural world for the next generation.

But this world still needs the Spirit. There remain the Bosnias, the Haitis, the alleyways of despair in every city. And how many unfired imaginations, locked doors of prejudice, and churches that claim God but lack love! There are still hearts that flounder because the meaning and the joy has gone out of commitment.

Come, Holy Spirit! Rouse and renew us! Set us free this very day! Unleash our voices for praise and our hearts for love!

HOLY ARE THE CARING
THE TRUSTWORTHY THE
BURDENED THE BROKEN-
HEARTED   holy holy holy
                    WHOLLY
AT HOME ARE YOU
IN THE *TRANS*
COM- *FORMED* ?
PANY
OF
GOD'S
FAITH-   ··················
FUL
THE   ROYALS
COM-
MUN-   ··················
ION OF
SAINTS   *WE ARE* **BORN** *TO IT*
              MADE AND **BAPTIZED**
       our god has taken up residence
       in a broken wounded humanity

       baptized royalty
                    treating the
hungrythenakedthejudged
thealienthedifferentthelonely
sadthedownontheirluck
thehomelesstheelders
        as royalty

1.

Wlat the Attic and Our Tradition Hold: Heroism, Holiness, and Heaven

Matthew 5:1-12

They say spirits live in the attic. I can attest to that since cleaning out the one in our family home in Milwaukee last weekend! I found, among other things, this ragged *Lives of the Saints* book, which my parents gave me when I was in grade school. Its legends about the great ones we remember today awakened my young imagination, gave me solid ideals, and probably influenced my vocational choice as well!

Saint bring to mind heroism, holiness, and heaven. First, saints are our Christian *heroes*. We need them, not more Hollywood or Superbowl heroes! They give us vision and values aligned with those of Jesus. They are heroes who are not perfect but who are admirably faithful. They aren't always the most talented of persons, but are always prayerful and giving ones! Some of these heroes are alive and some dead.

Just last week while visiting parishioners in the hospital, I said to one that the other was up on another floor. Irene responded, "That Lorraine is a real *saint!*" And that's how the Communion of Saints works: one person's quality of endurance gives another courage when needed. *Heroes* help us!

Saints are also *holy*. This means to me that they are grounded in God . . . not always patient and sometimes even stubborn, but grounded in the awareness of God's abiding presence. Thus, Jesus says in today's Gospel reading of the Sermon on the Mount, not "Blessed are the Somebodies," those successful 10's who panic and run from responsibility but maintain popularity, but rather "Holy are the caring, the real, the trustworthy, and yes, the burdened." Who of us isn't? And perhaps most poignant of all, "Blessed are the broken-hearted," those who hurt but don't give up on God.

Now the holy ones also include martyrs, whose beliefs took them the whole way home. If we were in El Salvador today perhaps that commitment would be asked of us. It's like the popular country song suggests, "You've got to stand for something, or you'll fall for anything!" Martyrs in our church are specially grounded in God to stand for God the whole way.

Finally, saints are experiencing *heaven*, we believe. We tend not to think much about how our belief in heaven affects our life here on earth. But that importance came to me about fifteen years ago when I was teaching high school and two of our girls committed suicide one Saturday night. On Monday morning, the principal asked all the teachers to help the students process their tragic loss of two classmates and friends. I found that the ones unable to be consoled were those who did not embrace a belief in the after-life. In other words, some of the kids thought their friends were finished. Done for. Period. Imagine if you would think that way when a loved one died!

The Communion of Saints is always something our people in R.C.I.A. ask about. The idea is very attractive. After all, it's a little bit of heaven right here on earth to be in the company of God's faithful ones. And heaven as home is an attractive idea, too. The only lasting one for us who are really only strangers here is the one we'll be welcomed to by the God Who invited us into this life in the first place!

To conclude, today is a harvest of Home-Coming for all God's faithful, saints canonized and unknown with whom we share a common call. The Good Spirits don't really live in the attic, or between the musty pages of this *Lives of the Saints* book. We can find them in the mirror, at our table, and among the clerks, waitresses, and gas station attendants we'll meet today.

So let's make a little bit of heaven on earth by our mercy, our bearing others' burdens, our disarming ways, even as we recall how much we've been given and forgiven! Today is the day to take the Halloween masks off and, like the jack-o-lantern, let the light shine through! I don't know about you, but "I want to be in that number when the saints go marching in!"

2.

How Meals Can Transform Us: Jesus' Table Fellowship Re-Played

Mark 14:12-16; 22-26

Some meals transform us. They change people. Last year, I asked our adults preparing for Easter sacraments to recall one meal that was a turning point for them. They shared about forgiveness extended because of a meal, eyes opened to another's goodness or hurt, commitments made, and dreams shaped . . . all because two or more people gathered, broke bread, and shared stories!

One contemporary theologian, John Shea, says that Christians are the ones whose strategy is to gather the folks, break the bread, and tell the stories! He says our nature, our heritage as a eucharistic people, is gleaned from a habit Jesus had: table fellowship, that is, teaching more often than not with His mouth full! Often in Scripture we find Jesus at table with all sorts of people who are hungry for more than food. In Jesus' company they are nourished. We see in these scenarios the early roots of our eucharistic life.

For centuries theologians quibbled about *just how* Jesus was present in the Eucharist. Was it physical? Symbolic? Finally, the word *really* was chosen to describe His sacramental presence. And when the Second Vatican Council came along and examined the sacred liturgy, a greater emphasis was also added to the *other* ways Jesus was present: in the Word of God proclaimed, in the presider and believing assembly, and in the meal shared. So the focus of Jesus' presence moved from the static to the dynamic dimension: from the elements of bread and wine to the people who gather in faith and the living message that also feeds us. And finally, that presence moves us into the culture in which we live and work as Body of Christ for our world. This broader understanding emphasizes how the *whole meal* transforms us as our lively faith makes it possible. *Interaction* is involved as we remember Jesus, are fed, and promise to share His mission.

Meals transform us. Who of us would accept an invitation to a banquet and then refuse to eat? Or be seated at a wedding dinner and choose not to converse? In today's Gospel, there is a strong mandate: Take! Eat! Take! Pass the cup! Share My life together! Learn what sacrificial love is about! And then, *become* what you eat and drink . . . the Body and Blood of Jesus for a starving and thirsty world. Become the ones who know how to share life, so Jesus' care can reach everyone.

How do we converse, interact, and partake at the eucharistic meal so as to be transformed? By greeting people in the assembly, responding to God's Word in song, speaking prayers for the needy, and pledging to be Christ's life for our world when we say Amen to His presence both in meal and assembly.

Years ago, we sang, "Oh Lord, I am not worthy" and as *sinful* creatures hardly dared encounter a *perfect* Lord. Today our eucharistic songs stress the gift Jesus' life is for us, and how hungry all the world is to be satisfied by Him alone. These hymns are about remembering His love and becoming His presence for others. The thrust is awe, nourishment, challenge, and transformation.

Once I attended a live production of *Jesus Christ Superstar*. One stage technique left a lasting impression: The gigantic table of the Last Supper became, in the next scene, *the World*, the arena of human activity, daily life. By some feat of art and technology, the space in which apostles had passed bread and wine became the world of trade and politics and human relations.

And it's in that progression that *our* transformation occurs! First we express faith, are nourished, form community and serve each other at the Eucharist. Then we are ready to touch the Body and Blood of Jesus in the fragile, the broken, and the needy all week. Then it's eucharist in the parking lot, hardware store, fast food restaurant, car dealership, city hall, and kitchen. These are the *ethical consequences* of participating in Eucharist. I *become* Christ's Body ground like wheat. I recognize His blood as you pour yourself out. Perhaps this is the transformation implied at the end of today's Gospel when it says that after they had drunk from the cup, they went out to the Mount of Olives. *That meal transformed them.*

Soon and Very Soon: Grand Finale for Those Waiting to See the King

Matthew 25:31-46

My mother was a heaven-seeker, as we are. She was born royalty: that is, made in God's image and baptized into the same royal family we are. And every time I hear our royal family's theme song, "Soon and Very Soon," I am transported to May of 1987, when my Mom was in a coma in a Milwaukee hospital and very near death. A friend and I stood on either side of her bed and sang quietly into her ears: "Soon and very soon, You are going to see the King!. . . . No more cryin' then . . . No more dyin' then. . . ." I was confident singing that because I knew she hadn't waited until *then* to meet our King; she'd known all along that the blessed are ones who've gotten familiar with the King as they responded to the needy.

Today's Gospel, like Mom's death, is a grand finale, this time for the end of our church year. It's a cosmic vision of judgment, with every nation gathered for the sorting and sifting. It doesn't resemble a Hall of Fame induction for V.I.P.'s, but rather a review of practical deeds performed for the right reasons. It's as if the royal family gathered there is reminded of their baptismal motto: "Include a hurting humanity now—or be excluded later" . . . or "Royalty who treat others as royalty will know the presence of the King sooner or later, in fact *forever*!"

What is being reviewed in that scene is a religion of practical deeds. Jesus had taken up residence in a wounded humanity and *there* was met, knowingly or unknowingly, by those who came close enough to touch. *Seeing* the King was that *soon*, that *often*, that *close*, and *that easy to miss*! The hurting had become, in this kingdom, the very *sacrament* of King Jesus! So the only sin is indifference, blindness, something like this:

- When I was a stranger, you forgot I was royalty . . .
  The King said, "I came as a German tourist and was killed in Miami just one hour after my arrival in America." But that's so far away. So the King says, "I was homeless in Saginaw and you weren't neighbor to me." And we reply, "Where, Jesus?" And He gets specific: "In places where residents refuse group homes into their neighborhoods. I could have been met there. You missed your King, and there's still crying now."

or

- When were you naked, Lord?
  He answers, "I was exposed and exploited by a ruthless newspaper which tried and convicted me by swaying public opinion before the facts of my alleged offense were out. My reputation and future were stripped from me." "But what could *we* have done?" we ask. "The press is bigger than all of us!" "You can make sure in your relationships to leave the judgments to me! Then you'll be blessed."

or

- An elated King will say, "There's less crying, less dying, because you served Me. When I was hungry in 1992, 140,000 people sent legislators letters regarding the "Every Fifth Child" bill. Some of you wrote last Lent at the soup supper. And as a result of baptized royalty treating the hungry as *royalty*, $900 million was added to WIC, Job Corps, and Head Start. I was hungry in every fifth child, and you fed the King."

And on and on the scenarios could go.

Each church year the circle of God's reign gets wider because people like us, heaven-seekers, serve and often *see* the

King as we commit ourselves to seeing that there's less crying, less dying, among God's royal people. *We don't have to wait to see the King!* Advent begins a new year of meeting Him in Word, sacrament, and service. One thing is certain: As we pray "Thy kingdom come," we don't have to wait. It's *soon! Very soon!* Alleluia!

shark tissue can cure infection;
the fish we most fear
may destroy the
disease we
most
fear

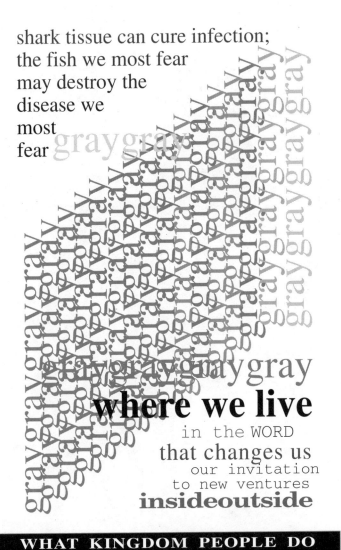

where we live
in the WORD
that changes us
our invitation
to new ventures
insideoutside

WHAT KINGDOM PEOPLE DO

1.

Staying Haunted by the Relics

Matthew 10:26-33

We need to stay haunted by the *relics*! I have here my Dad's old pipe, a reminder of the one-liners he came out with while smoking it. I recalled them and recorded all I could remember after he died because they summarize his message, his advice, and his personality. I wanted them to guide me the second half of *my* life. They deal with the need of God, the importance of feeding hungry children, and support for the poor.

As an assembly of Jesus' sisters and brothers, we are haunted by *another* sacred relic: The Word of God, the collected sayings of the Savior Who guides our communal life. Today we heard a piece from Matthew directed at greenhorns, disciples about to be trained as missionaries. They are recent converts to Christianity from Judaism, have undergone persecution for it, and are having an identity crisis because they lost their Temple and are under siege much the way today's missionaries in Central America are. So Jesus is reported to have given them advice, warnings, and loving reassurance.

What unites Matthew's sayings is the theme of "Do not be afraid!" It appears three times and illustrates Jesus' understanding of human nature. We fear pain and He knows that so well!

Imagine if we were to list all the fears we encounter in one weekend. I had six, but really, only three were related to the *cost of discipleship*. All the rest were anxieties like "Will I get lost trying to find that place?" Or "It's slippery; I could fall off this bike!"

What do *disciples* fear? First, that the Good News will be received as bad news. Take this verse: "What you hear in the dark, tell in the daylight." I used to think it meant crime, shame and lust will be seen. Yet what about the intimate whispers of prayer made in the dark, the private times of praise and thanks? These need to come to light, too! One recent interpretation I heard of this verse is that the number who will hear Jesus' teachings from His *own* lips will be few, but the number that will hear them from the future disciples is many. So that *bad* news is really *good*!

A second thing that disciples fear is that the consequences of proclaiming the message will be negative. The risk factor seems high. Where will this commitment to Jesus lead me? Opposition? Loss of friends? One time I remember saying, "Lord, I'll do anything for You *except* sing solo at a microphone and beg for money." *Guess what I've done the past year in my pastoral ministry*? But they both helped get the message out, the first with psalms as cantor and the second by obtaining scholarship monies for our youth. Yes, the risk factor does *stretch* us as disciples! And yes, when we preach Jesus' message unaltered, some walk away. But if we lose no friends because we are His friends, I don't know if the message was spoken loudly enough!

Finally, a third fear factor for the disciple: Can we really trust that *good* is more powerful than *evil*? I thought of this last Saturday when I read about two activities going on at the same time in our city: the gun show and the annual "Bike for Life"!

Yet believers in the Gospel must know that God's Spirit can touch human hearts in ways never imagined. This came to mind recently when I read that researchers have discovered shark tissue can cure infections, even cancer in some cases. The fish we most fear may destroy the disease we most dread! God can use even the most fearsome creatures for healing!

Such harsh teachings as "Turn the other cheek" and "Love your enemies" may alienate some listeners, but watered down, they distort Jesus' challenge. Though we enjoy legal religious freedom, beliefs we hold may still be attacked, but our suffering for them is a cost of discipleship. The perk for missionaries, however, is that Jesus promises a close watch on our lives, so close even the hair on our head is counted! Now on this divine involvement we rely at every turn!

A wonderful theologian, Walter Brueggeman, has said, "Serious speech by trusted people can change the world." My Dad's words have changed me. And Jesus' words are changing *us*. Our Baptism called us to the long haul for an enterprise worth our life's effort. We now re-commit ourselves to the mission of Jesus by reciting our parish mission statement as today's creed.

2.

Choosing the Roller Coaster, Not the Merry-Go-Round

Mark 1:14-20

A little girl in Saginaw had been taught to pray very hard that the United States would not go to war in the Persian Gulf. She did just that. So on that famous Wednesday when she heard President Bush declare war, she called her grandmother and asked, "Grandma, what do I pray for *tonight*?"

We witnessed the historic destruction of the Berlin Wall not many years ago and were euphoric, watching the world lean toward what seemed to be a peace within reach. But then came violence in South Africa, turmoil in the Baltic States, war in the Persian Gulf, and on and on the list goes.

Where were you when war was declared on January 16th? Probably doing what you ordinarily do on Wednesday nights: finishing the dinner dishes, taking your child to a music lesson, telephoning a friend, getting the homework started, or watching the news. And that *news* called you out of the ordinary into changes.

Jesus issues a call to ordinary people in ordinary circumstances of life in today's Gospel. These fishermen were apparently successful, judging from the boats they owned and their hired help. They had little reason to change. Business was steady enough and they had already heard of the opposition to this man Jesus. But his challenge attracted them. They became disciples, and the two requirements were faith and reform: *belief* . . . and the *change* that follows. The Good News Jesus broadcast was that God's reign would be achieved, but only when ordinary people changed their hearts.

Let's move from Galilee to Saginaw with this invitation. We were called at baptism and are invited continuously to discipleship. This means faith and change. Remember, the little girl whose prayer changed still had her eyes on Jesus!

We don't tend to choose change. Even when we know we should diet, join AA, or give up a grudge, we hesitate. Most often, change is thrust upon us by circumstance. I remember reflecting how the Gulf War and Jesus' invitation to change intersected.

Jesus' call to change meant an examination of our notions:

- of *success*: Was victory watching a manipulative leader in Iran disarmed, *or* working toward a wholeness in the human family that would be universal and lasting?
- of *parenting*: Was it more important to buy our children the war toys they wanted, *or* to model for them cooperation and sharing among the neighbors?
- of *relating*: Was friendship getting what I could from people *or* appreciating differences and learning from them?

Everyone who followed Jesus had to leave something. They also had to embrace new responsibilities because of the new vision they had. Embracing change requires courage. Recently I asked a group beginning a new venture in discipleship what their fears were. They said not knowing enough, the time commitment, and maybe not saying the right thing. These fears are no different from the disciples'. But the invitation to new ventures is coming from One Who thinks the world of us, and intimacy with Him brings the help needed. For in this venture of following, we need a Savior more than a missile detector, for our belief is in the God Who wants no city destroyed!

A few days ago, I watched the video *Parenthood* starring Steve Martin and Jason Robards. In it an old woman most people think is too foolish to make any real sense gives some wise advice to a struggling middle-aged couple. I think it's good advice for those of us wanting to answer the call to discipleship as well. She says you can live life either on a roller coaster or on a merry-go-round. The merry-go-round is safer because it repeats the same motion without getting anywhere. But the roller coaster, while a riskier ride, is amazing as well as frightening, and the ups and downs, when taken with someone who loves you, is really an exciting adventure.

Welcome to the roller coaster of discipleship!

Welcome the Child . . . Or Forfeit Sitting in the Lap of God!

Mark 9:30-37

Would everyone here who is striving to be a faithful disciple of Jesus raise your hand? I can see we're in good company! As disciples, one of our main tasks is to listen to the words of the Master in an attentive way. And the Word from Him today focuses on "welcoming the child." That's not so easy!

What was the context for this? For Jesus to welcome a child into the rabbinical teaching circle was radical. It was unheard of for a rabbi to welcome women *or* children in that time. In Aramaic, the word for "child" and "servant" was the same. Rabbis would never acknowledge or value them. To say "child" was to mean a nobody, a powerless one, the lowest in status and importance. Thus when He said "Welcome the child," Jesus meant "Raise the lowly."

In the other Gospels, Jesus goes so far as to suggest we *become* like children. But even when He only says to *welcome* the child, what happens to its meaning? It is often misused and sentimentalized. Some think, "Isn't it cute?" and others take it to mean we can be irresponsible or immature because Jesus says it's OK.

A refreshing and challenging way we might interpret "Welcome the child" is to apply it to *our* child, within. Can we search for and befriend, get to know and invite out, that hurt, quiet, unacknowledged one inside who desires to learn, to explore, to play, to articulate what might delight and surprise us? That child needs to be acknowledged and celebrated today!

And what can we learn from the child about holiness? About discipleship? Three scenarios follow, each with one lesson.

- My nephew Dave was in first grade and had one of those workbooks with a circle in which he was supposed to copy the same number of dots that appeared in the circle across the page. After he had successfully done that, I asked, "What are those?" to which he answered, "Aunt Jane! Those are chocolate chips!" How grateful I was he didn't answer "Coins" or "Computer chips"! The child sees possibility where we see boredom, routine, the expected outcome.

- On a recent day off, my roommate and I went on a series of "neighborhood bakery" tours! We had long spoken of this as a favorite fantasy, but one day took a thermos of coffee, butter and knife, and map of the locations of family-owned bakeries. We visited six in a morning, taking turns picking out one item in each place to share in a park before the next visit! We certainly weren't acting productive or professional; in fact, I have seldom had a greater sense of sabbath leisure! But we had every reason to let our inner child take delight, and could praise God at day's end for fantasy-turned-reality!

- One of my friends got word that her father had died earlier that morning, but that the nursing home had kept him there until she arrived. I went with her for this most unusual farewell. My friend is known for her competent presence, so to see her at his bedside was a rare and mystifying experience. She spoke to him tenderly, aloud, like a child at prayer. There was no "Gimme," no "Why me?" but only affection and gratitude, trust and honesty ... all expressed with a simplicity that was most endearing! We need to pray like children.

In conclusion, when Jesus said to welcome the child, did He mean we should do what we can about coke and crack babies in our day? I think so. Did He hope we would find a simple, spontaneous, and creative way to live? Yes! And did He mean that we should pray with affect? I believe so. For if we do, we can hope to sit in God's lap for eternity!

4.

CAESAR AND CHARLIE BROWN: FACING THE GRAY AREAS

Matthew 22:15-21

There is a Peanuts comic strip which shows Lucy at the 5¢ advice booth and Charlie Brown a confused client. He can't find direction in his life. She suggests he imagine life as an ocean liner. Some face their deck chairs toward the bow, and some toward the side or back. Which, she asks, does he choose? "I can't unfold my chair!" he complains. For Charlie Brown, life isn't simply choosing option A or B. In fact, our lives aren't that simple, either. The older I become, the more gray area I see, and not only at my temples!

In today's Gospel, Jesus undergoes a test and is offered options A and B like Charlie. But both answers are a trap. It's a no-win situation and He knows it. If He answers that yes, they should pay the tax to Caesar, He will be accused of being a Roman sympathizer. If no, He'll be perceived as a subversive agitator. So he answers A and B, and when they show Him a Roman coin, he knows they'd intended to pay no matter what, because shekels weren't used for taxes! Jesus breaks out of the trap by stating the simple truth: I won't choose either/or. Life's gray areas make it more complicated than that. It is a both/ and reality.

Similar dilemmas face Jesus' followers, on whose faces the Creator's image is imprinted. And God won't remove us from the world of struggle and decision. So what does the Gospel message compel us to do in the face of hard questions, the gray areas? Certainly not be satisfied with a simple A or B response!

The answers arise from study, prayer, and conversation as we discover the complexity and excitement of trying to wed our two citizenships: relating to culture and loyalty to Creator. As believers, we look at the Stock Exchange, Dow, the U.N., GM, the YMCA, NBC, K-Mart, college tuition, and fluctuating interest rates through eyes of faith. Vatican II reminded Christians that they could not separate their faith from their cultural milieu. We can't remain aloof from questions of war technology, medical ethics, and consequences of capitalism. But how to apply the values of Jesus isn't immediately clear as we face global complexities of profit, production, international markets, and the poor at home. What is clear is that to those whose hearts have the imprint of the Creator, all *creation* matters. And all *the created* matter.

Now if Jesus were confronted by a mob of questioners today, they would not be Pharisees or Herod in the Temple courtyard in Jerusalem. They would be call-ins to a television talk show or New Englanders attending a town meeting or folks like us at a grand opening of a Chevy dealer. We'd be in the crowd or on the call-in line asking about the gray areas of our day: the struggles that would be no struggles at all if we'd just accommodate our faith to our culture and *fit in*! Or if we'd compromise our beliefs to achieve quick success.

Some of the questions *we'd* ask would sound like: Can my corporation continue to enjoy this profit margin without resorting to hiring south of the border for less? How can we keep benefiting from this river without polluting it? And the kids might wonder, How can I make and keep these friends if I can't buy designer clothes? And the weary, very marrieds might ask, How can our love withstand the strain that family demands place on it?

And Jesus' answer at the town hall meeting and on the talk show and at the grand opening is the same: I gave you freedom; I have no blueprint. In the kingdom, one size does not fit all.

Talk alone is cheap, and lip service can be little more than hypocrisy. He would probably agree with President Clinton's appraisal: "America's freedom *of* religion does not mean freedom *from* religion." And He would reiterate God's mere tolerance of government or diocesan bureaucracy as a way to meet human needs. He would smile on taxpayers who demand accountability from those who spend tax monies and electors who insist on ethical performance from those elected.

The *image* on our coins is a President's head. But the words read, "In *God* we trust." So there's no longer the sacred and the secular, this world and the other, either/or. Faith and culture are joined in a rich but often confusing blend of beauty and pain, greed and giving, by those of us with both citizenships. This tension and challenge, grace and call, began at our baptism, for it is the baptized who bear God's own life into the culture with all its broken promises, moral ambiguity, and great faith. And inside the security of God's provident care, we continue to struggle with the *gray areas* of this earthly pilgrimage, fed here with heavenly food as we travel into the both/and!

5.

Standing By Jesus, Our God-Send

John 6:60-69

There are times we walk away from people because we realize we don't understand them, and probably never will. There are other times we walk away from people because we understand them perfectly well—and what their truth demands of us seems unbearable, unthinkable, *beyond us* at the moment, or maybe forever! And then—and then—there are times we think we can neither understand nor tolerate someone's truth, but out of love, out of deep loyalty, we stand by. . . even for a lifetime . . . and find affection, meaning, joy, and a profound mercy.

Now the only Person each one of us holds in common is Jesus, so let's refer all of these scenarios to today's Gospel, to His person and mission. In retrospect, we name Him a "God-send" and are here because we are committed, like Peter, despite not always understanding and sometimes struggling to respond to His truth.

When Jesus says "Eat My flesh" in today's Gospel passage, and many former disciples decide they're not about to stay with a cannibal, this isn't the *first* time Jesus stumped them with riddles that are pretty hard to take seriously. And every time, His truth divides the community down the middle because it forces a decision. After all, He's already mentioned loving your enemy, turning the other (as yet unslapped) cheek, not trusting too much in material things, and making sure you're last now, so you'll be first later! Who but a God-send could be in His right mind—in His right *heart*—and have the authority to demand those?

Peter answers that at the end of our Good News message today: "I have come to know that You are the Holy One of God." There is the *identity* of the one with authority to ask what seems impossible. But first there was the murmuring, the doubt, the struggle. This just wasn't natural!

Peter had not been without skepticism. And neither are we. Non-violent responses to violence done to us don't come easily. Generous responses to selfish overtures are not natural. And not being overly impressed by *stuff* demands a holiness we strive for all our lives. Peter says, "I have come to know Who You are, Jesus . . ." not "I always knew You, my fishing friend!" And not everyone was up to what was being asked. Some left the challenge to Peter. Others saw where all this would lead and got out while there was still time. And some? Some *just loved Him.* Some simply took the leap and didn't go away.

One of the deepest human experiences, and one shared by nearly all people, is a fear of abandonment. Jesus, Son of God, God-send, was not spared that experience. His words "Will you also leave Me?" must have haunted Peter, who really did not understand Jesus, nor tolerate His challenges, much better than his buddies on the beach. But he leaped to Jesus' side out of love.

And we? We know things aren't so clear: *How* can His flesh be life for the world? *How* can we really be His Body and Blood for the hungry and hopeless? But *that* we love Him enough to risk staying, *that* we come here to re-pledge ourselves to His puzzling but adventuresome reign, is enough reason to celebrate Eucharist in loving memory of Him. Because when we *love* enough, we can put up with a lot of *unsolvables*!

And after all, if not to Jesus, *where would we turn*?

Index to Lectionary for Sundays and Solemnities